Live Smart
Start Young

Jump start your life.

Stand out from the competition.

Build your future.

Michael W. Miller

ISBN 978-0-692-68445-0

Published by: Live Smart, Start Young, LLC
www.livesmartstartyoung.com
333 S. Tamiami Trail #205
Venice FL, 34285

Cover designed by: Victoria Dietz, Studio V Gallery
Edited by: Bernadette Miller Stocking
Printed By: Steve The Printer

Dedication

This book is dedicated to my son, Michael (Fish), and to my other seven children before him, Beau, Tamara, Victoria, Mariah, Ryan, Cody and Dylan. Michael completed high school in 2016 and is embarking on the same voyage as his siblings and many others his age. I wish them all smooth sailing. My hope is that they find success and strength to become their best.

Acknowledgments

To my loving wife, Tammy, who remained patient and positive and persevered with me to complete our first addition of Live Smart, Start Young. To my daughter, Victoria, who supported and assisted with our book. To the memory of my Uncle Bill, who shared his library and his Boston Whaler during my vacation to the Florida Keys at age sixteen. This experience set the direction of my sail.

To all the professional motivational speakers who have spent countless hours researching and sharing their life experiences, many of whom continue to inspire me. Their teachings are shared throughout this book.

When all else fails, it is my belief in God that comforts me. My deepest thanks to Tammy for supporting me in my faith journey. After all, in the face of the impossible, it is faith that moves one through life's challenges. In the face of every up and down, we are in God's hands. I hope you discover this early.

Table of Contents

Introduction

I hope this book helps Michael, his siblings and others of all ages to have a better understanding of their purposes in life, to clearly see what is important to them, and to be rewarded for their efforts. This book describes the beginning of an ongoing experience. The joy is in the process. At each plateau, we find new endeavors to conquer. As we grow and succeed, our destinations expand. They are infinite.

The world continues to be competitive and complicated. People of every age are looking for quick answers and easy solutions to these challenges. There are many experiences in a lifetime, and this book is purposely written from experience to bring you success in several aspects of life. It focuses on saving you time and energy in specific ways to bring happiness and satisfaction to your life.

Each topic is addressed briefly, includes a conclusion and a quote and is often followed by an anecdote from my life and the lives of my mentors, family and friends. I urge you to launch your own exploration on each of the topics and come to your own conclusions. My wish is that these topics become a compass for you throughout your life.

Throughout the pages, you will find places to take notes and write down thoughts. You may want to keep track of books to read. Please keep a copy of this book throughout your journey in your life so that you can refresh your thoughts, beliefs and personal philosophy. Over time, things will certainly change, and your priorities will change too.

Topic Index

- What to expect when you are responsible for earning an income to cover your living expenses.

- How to determine what income you need to support your desired lifestyle.

- Choosing to maximize your brain's potential.

- Positive thoughts, positive talk, positive actions and positive people are crucial to make life most rewarding.

- The importance of finding your purpose in life. Staying hungry to remain at the top of your profession.

- Get what you want in life by helping others get what they want.

- You are solely responsible for your life, no matter where you start or where you are now.

- What you believe is what affects your life the most.

- You have to put yourself first then you can help others.

- Failure can be your friend.

- There are many resources to help you navigate the jungle.

- Understanding taxes you will be paying.

One
Why Young? Why Now?

Why start now, when you are young? Why not? Why wait? Sometimes you answer a question with a question. Why live 10 years or 20 years to learn some simple truths that can save time, money and heartache? These ideas can provide you more quality time in your life and less down time. There is no reason to wait.

Conclusion
It's never too late, but why not now?"

Quotes
It's easier to build strong children than to repair broken men.
Frederick Douglass

Good habits formed at youth make all the difference.
Aristotle

Yesterday is not ours to recover, but tomorrow is ours to win or loose.
Lyndon B. Johnson

Personal Experience
Thanks to my father who taught me excellent work habits, (something I did not realize at the time) and my supervisors and mentors Jack Brenner (a former Marine), and Charlie Plumb (a former employer), I was fortunate to have tremendous opportunity at a young age. I moved to Houston after graduating from college in Tampa at 21 years old.

Tampa was in a recession in 1977 and Houston was booming. My career started in construction management and after three years at age 25, I started my own construction/development business. I earned my first million dollars, only to give most of it back during the recession in 1982. My first big life lesson was that things that go up can quickly

3

come down.

A few years later, as the president of a public company at age 30, I continued to gain tremendous experience and had many opportunities that proved vital for my future. (I became a member of the Young Presidents Club.)

It pays to start early in life because there will be setbacks that you will encounter, setbacks that will test your determination. Starting young will give you time to recover from your setbacks.

Recommended Book

Awaken the Giant Within
Tony Robbins

NOTES

_____

_____

_____

_____

_____

_____

_____

_____

_____

_____

_____

_____

_____

_____

_____

_____

_____

Two
Why and What Is Success?

Success is different for each of us. You will choose your own definition of success. It can change over time. It will be in such areas as wealth, health, friendships, relationships, employment and spiritual well-being. Thousands of books are, and will continue, to be written about success.

One dictionary's definition of success is, "the accomplishment of an aim or purpose."

Conclusion
Success in many areas of life is important and should not be neglected. Determine what success is for you in several areas, such as wealth, health, friendships, relationships, employment and spiritual well-being.

Quotes
Success is doing what you enjoy in life and getting paid for it!
Les Brown

Success is something you attract not something you pursue.
Jim Rohn

Success is not final. Failure is not fatal. It's the courage to continue that counts.
Winston Churchill

Success without successors is a failure.
Unknown

Personal Experience
Although I have enjoyed many successes in my business endeavors and some setbacks too, the jury is still out! By that, I mean with each achievement I have realized there is always more one can accomplish. I was most gratified throughout life when I accomplished more than I set out to do. I feel this has occurred in business and in my personal life too. Adopting my oldest son and two daughters at ages 3, 5 and 7 has always and will always give me tremendous satisfaction and a feeling of accomplishment. To have the opportunity to give and receive from

three strangers with whom I fell in love, and to have them love me back is a lifetime achievement, for me - for anyone.

A few years later, I was fortunate to have two birth children! Wow, a boy and a girl. How perfect. Raising them from diapers was something new. Having three older siblings, they received some real loving. Then, with five children, I felt very fortunate and my life was filled with joy, much love and many great times!

Just after thinking I had reached the top, I became the stepfather of three young men! Now with eight kids from 17 to 33 years old, I have new horizons to conquer.

To me success is accomplishing more than you ever imagined and helping others do the same. I am not through yet.

Recommended Books

The ABC's of Success
Bob Proctor

Outliers - The Story of Success
Malcom Gladwell

NOTES

_____

_____

_____

_____

_____

_____

_____

_____

_____

_____

_____

Three
Determining Your Purpose in Life

Not everyone knows his or her purpose in life. Perhaps that is why some people are not as motivated as others are. Purpose gives you a reason to get up early in the morning and stay up late in the evening. Purpose eliminates work. Pursuing your purpose is fun. Purpose saves lives. It can help you live healthier, happier and wiser. If you are unaware of your purpose in life, it is okay. Now is the time to search for it. Over time, it may change, but finding your purpose in life is critical.

Living without a purpose leaves you in a cloud of uncertainty. It leaves you without the fuel that propels you forward. Consequently, you will fall farther behind.

Conclusion
Strive to find your purpose in life because it will help you reach great achievements, have positive self-esteem and enjoy your life.

Quotes
To succeed, you need to find something to hold on to, something to motivate you, something to inspire you.
Tony Dorsett

The two most important days of your life are the day you were born and the day you realize why you were born.
Mark Twain

You don't get to choose how or when you're going to die. You can only decide how you're going to live.
Joan Baez

Personal Experience
Finding my purpose in life is something that I never consciously pursued or was quite aware of. I always had goals and wanted to be successful, but never tried to answer the question, "What is my purpose in life." I believe, however, that I always asked myself, "What can I do with my time that is important?" My purpose was to support my family, and later it became to help others find a home that they would love and live in

through their retirement years. Then I worked to provide business offices for companies in which they could operate and grow. As time moved on, my purpose included enhancing the lives of my employees, by not only providing them a job, but to help them become more than they ever thought they could be -To help them seek their dreams and their life ambitions.

Now I am attempting to share ideas, thoughts, beliefs and experiences with young adults to help you get a jump-start in transitioning from being young adults to adulthood and from being primarily dependent on their parents or guardians to becoming personally and financially independent.

Recommended Books

Live Your Dreams
Les Brown

Purpose Driven Life
Rick Warren

NOTES

Four
It Is All about You

It is all about you, although you may not be feeling or thinking that way. You are the architect of your life, not your parents, siblings, teachers, friends or the government, just you. You are responsible for your life, its successes and its failures. You are the only one who can change you; nobody else can. You are accountable for your life; no one else is. Blaming others will get you nowhere. Your history, environment, nationality, sex, race, financial condition, and your education all have one thing in common. They will not determine what you choose to do with your life. You have the ability to change yourself and move beyond any situation that impedes your efforts to become the person you want to be.

Conclusion
What you get out of your life is controlled by you.

Quotes
There are no constraints on the human mind, no walls around the human spirit and no barriers to our progress, except those we construct ourselves.
Ronald Reagan

Isn't it ironic that the only person who can make you really happy is the same person who makes you sad and lonely?
HpLyrikz /Tumblr

Life is not about finding yourself. It's about creating yourself.
George Bernard Shaw

You could make a wish or you could make it happen!
Unknown

Read the flight of your arrow if you want to know your future.
Alessandro Baricco

Accept responsibility for your life. Know that it is you who will get you where you want to go, no one else.
Les Brown

Personal Experience

I met Harry Bruns in 1978 in Houston, Texas in a small office building where he operated his oil drilling business for more than 45 years. Mr. Bruns served in the Marine Corp and shared many stories about his service overseas and his many years drilling for oil. He explained that it was not always a sure bet when he selected a spot to drill, but he had his share of lucky strikes, as he called them. He claimed that luck always followed lots of research and many years of hard work.

After learning about his life story, he gave me a copy of his creed that he proudly hung on his office wall. It was, "I do not choose to be a common man." I have it hanging on my wall in my office today. I have lived my life believing in this creed and reading it often. Everybody needs his or her own creed to live by.

Recommended Books

Life Is What You Make It
Peter Buffet

Unlimited Power
Anthony Robbins

NOTES

_____

_____

_____

_____

_____

_____

_____

_____

_____

_____

My Creed

Compliments of Harry Bruns

I do not choose to be a common man.
It is my right to be uncommon … if I can.
I seek opportunity … not security.
I do not wish to be a kept citizen,
Humbled and dulled by having the State look after me.
I want to take the calculated risk,
To dream and to build.

To fail and to succeed.
I refuse to barter incentive for a dole;
I prefer the challenges of life to the guaranteed existence;
The thrill of fulfillment to the stale calm of Utopia.
I will not trade freedom for beneficence
Nor my dignity for a handout
I will never cower before any master
Nor bend to any threat.
It is my heritage to stand erect, proud and unafraid;
To think and act for myself,
To enjoy the benefit of my creations
And to face the world boldly and say:
This, with God's help, I have done.
All this is what it means to be an Entrepreneur.

Excerpted from Common Sense, written in 1776,
by Thomas Paine

Five
Work Hard on Yourself

Work hard at your job, but really work hard on yourself. Most people overlook where his or her efforts should be directed. They work hard at their job, work hard at home, and work hard on their relationships. First and foremost, you should work hard on yourself, so that you constantly improve.

You can improve your mind, your health, your personality, your communication skills, your ability to be patient and your ability to be positive. When you do, all areas of your life are lifted. Your life will become more productive, more meaningful, and you will experience more pleasure and most importantly, more pleasure in those around you.

Conclusion
Spend time on yourself. It's not selfish. It's beneficial to everyone you love and care about.

Quotes
Let him who would move the world first move himself.
Socrates

Hard work beats talent when talent doesn't work hard.
Tim Notke

Formal education will make you a living;
Self-education will make you a fortune.
Jim Rohn

Personal Experience
My father tried to get me to read something every day, but I failed to take his advice until I was 16 years old. It was then I became aware of several motivational speakers and professional coaches, including Dale Carnegie, Norman Vincent Peale, Tony Robbins, Jim Rohn, Zig Zigler and many others. Over the years, I have attended several motivational seminars. This includes walking on hot coals with Tony Robbins and 2,000 other pumped up success-searching individuals. I have never spent a lot of time on personal health, but I did run a 26-mile marathon

in Honolulu in 1980 at 25 years old.

It was only recently that I realized it is not selfish to work on yourself; it is your responsibility to do so.

Recommended Book

Success is a State of Mind
Les Brown

NOTES

_____

_____

_____

_____

_____

_____

_____

_____

_____

_____

_____

_____

_____

_____

_____

_____

_____

_____

_____

_____

_____

_____

Six
It Is Lonely At The Top

We all have heard the saying, "It's lonely at the top." There are fewer people at the top. This will never change. Not everyone will choose to move to the top. It is a choice. So the sooner you understand what it takes to raise to the top the better, if you choose to be there.

For instance, there is no exact science or law that guarantees rising or staying at the top of your game or profession. Constant hard work and self-improvement moves you toward the top. Competition and life's challenges will try to take you down from the top. There is not room for everybody at the top. It is unfortunate, but true. So do not take it for granted if you get there.

Conclusion
If you rise to the top, you must embrace the sacrifices that are required to maintain your position. Major achievement is brief if not constantly pursued.

Quotes
You must be willing to do the things today that others won't do in order to have the things tomorrow others won't have.
Les Brown

Personal Experience
I have been working for 44 years in the real estate development business, with much help from others. I built a company with more than 140 employees and annual revenues that exceeded $100 million. I realize that although I have been fortunate to go places, meet a variety of people, experience many wonderful things and spend considerable time with my family, there have been times that I experienced loneliness being at the top of my profession.

Many people do not know what it's like or have not had the opportunity to experience it. Therefore, many people may not relate to the challenges and sacrifices that one experiences at the top of their profession. This includes the perseverance that is required, the feeling of not letting others down, and the difficulties of constantly moving forward or facing the results from falling behind. With all this in mind, there is no better place to be if it is truly what you want. Of course, there are many benefits, but it is not for everyone.

Recommended Book

You Have a Brain
Ben Carson, M.D.

NOTES

_____

_____

_____

_____

_____

_____

_____

_____

_____

_____

_____

_____

_____

_____

_____

_____

_____

_____

_____

_____

_____

_____

_____

_____

Seven
Who Is At The Top?

There is no particular type individual that becomes wealthy, healthy or successful and ends up at the top. There is no type person that reaches his or her goals and lands at the top of their profession.

Poor people become wealthy. Sick people become healthy. Healthy people become sick. Rich people become poor. One can become the other.

People who reach their goals or end up at the top are the ones that believe they can. Those that find their purpose in life, those that are not afraid to face their fears, and those that learn from their failures often are the ones that reach their goals and reach the top. Those who learn that giving more than they receive will move closer to the top. In addition, it never hurts to attract some luck along the way.

Conclusion
There is no excuse for you to not make it to the top if that is what you want to do. It is that simple. In order to get there, you will need to believe, "It is worth it." People, who do not reach their goals, or turn from pursuing them, make the decision that "It's not worth it." Therefore, when you decide, "It's worth it," you have to go for it!

Quotes
Don't stop until you reach the top. When you reach the top don't stop, keep moving up.
Constance Chucks Friday

There's room at the top because so few are willing to pay the extra price to get there.
Ritchie Norton

Personal Experience
When I read the book, *See You at the Top*, by Zig Ziglar, I learned what it would take to get to get to the top. The steps are:
- Self-image
- Your relationships with others

- Your goals
- Your attitude
- Your work and desire

These steps take you to the top of the stairway to:
- Love
- Opportunity
- Leisure
- Security
- Peace
- Happiness
- Money
- Health
- Growth and friends

The handrails that assist you in your destination are:
- Loyalty
- Honesty
- Character
- Faith
- Integrity

Using these teachings has helped me through my life because they make so much sense. Once understood, they can be extremely helpful.

Personally, I like most people I meet who are at the top. We learn a lot from them. That does not mean that they don't have faults or that they have all the answers. However, learning from those that have accomplished things that are similar to those things you may want to achieve can only increase your chances and lessen the time required to get there. Some do not stay at the top, but I learned from them too. Remember what goes up can certainly come down.

Before you decide to go to the top, you have to decide, "It is worth it." Failing to make this decision will result in turning back as the challenges occur and the pain is increased.

Once you decide, "It's worth it, the challenges will be overcome and the pain will not last.

Recommended Book

See You at the Top
Zig Ziglar

NOTES

Eight
Your Health

Everyone knows that we can live longer and perhaps happier if we are in good health. What we often do not do however, is be healthy in small ways and in small steps. For example, walk five minutes a day to begin, sacrifice one bad food, eliminate one meal per week (not breakfast), find a drink that we can do without, and replace it with water.

We gain weight and break down our bodies in small steps. Why not repair and improve in small ways and in small steps.

Conclusion
Take small steps to improve and maintain your health.

Quotes
Health is not a condition of matter, but of mind.
Mary Baker Eddy

If you treat wellness with conviction, you will need less time to treat your illnesses.
Unknown

Personal Experience
Although I have not always been actively practicing good health, (for example I have consumed a lot of alcohol and carbohydrates through the years), I have been fortunate to enjoy good health. I have not had any serious illnesses, at least not yet. As you get older of course, your metabolism slows down and you add weight from fewer calories than previously consumed. Other health issues arise. You should anticipate PWO (parts wearing out).

I have known several people who neglected their health only to become ill or to die at a young age. Others just have had bad luck. There is nothing to prevent an illness or death.

Just hope you do not find yourself in the first category.

Recommended Book

The Seasons of Life
Jim Rohn

NOTES

_____

_____

_____

_____

_____

_____

_____

_____

_____

_____

_____

_____

_____

_____

_____

_____

_____

_____

_____

_____

_____

_____

_____

_____

_____

_____

Nine
Change Who?

No one can change you. If you want to change, you have to change yourself. Others can give you great advice and be great examples for your change. The sooner you realize it is your responsibility if you want to change, the quicker you will take the necessary steps to do so.

In addition, people spend so much time trying to change others. It is not likely that you will be successful in changing others until and unless they want to change.

Conclusion
Spend your efforts on changing yourself and not others. Your example may prove more beneficial to others than your advice would.

Quotes
Never believe that a few caring people can't change the world. For, indeed that is all whoever has.
Margaret Mead

When we are no longer able to change a situation, we are challenged to change ourselves.
Viktor E. Frankl
Author of Man's Search for Meaning

If you will change, everything will change for you.
Jim Rohn

Personal Experience
When I accepted the fact that if I wanted different results from my actions I had to change, then I got different results. When I have wanted others to change, I stood waiting. When I have told others that it is up to them to change, that nobody could change them, and that they had to want to change, only then did I see others change.

Recommended Books

Who Moved My Cheese?
Spencer Johnson, M.D.

Getting Unstuck
Pema Chodron

NOTES

_____

_____

_____

_____

_____

_____

_____

_____

_____

_____

_____

_____

_____

_____

_____

_____

_____

_____

_____

_____

_____

_____

_____

Ten
Who Is The Captain Of Your Ship?

Every ship needs a captain. It is your choice to become the captain or to pick someone to be your captain. Your voyage as well as your destination will be determined by your choices. If it is not your choice, others will make it for you.

Conclusion
Accept the responsibility to be the captain of your ship knowing you will go through rough waters. You will be pleased with your outcome because it will be who you are and who you have become. Each wave will make you better.

Quotes
When you think everything is someone else's fault, you will suffer a lot. When you realize that everything springs only from yourself, you will learn both peace and joy.
His Holiness the 14th Dalai Lama

All of us are self-made, but only the successful admit it.
Earl Nightingale

Personal Experience
I have owned boats all my life. Although I have never had a captain's license, I took charge of my vessel. I accepted my responsibility, which is the safety of the crew on board my vessel. In life, we must assume the role of captain of our own ship because we are responsible for our lives and those of our crew. No one else can assume that responsibility.

During the summer of 2014, I hired Capt. Joe Petrucco to take myself and three of my sons, Beau, Cody and Michael from Islamorada, Florida to the island of Bimini and Chub Cay in the Bahamas. Capt. Joe had made the trip several times and knew where the great fishing was in the blue waters of the Caribbean. Even though I put my trust in Capt. Joe to run the 37-foot Sea Hunter across the jet stream and get us home safely, I never delegated my responsibility to be in charge of our lives at sea.

Recommended Book

The Road to Your Best Stuff
Mike William

NOTES

Eleven
Career Choices,
Income and Expense Summary

There are many exciting and rewarding careers and lifestyles. It is important to understand the rewards and different gratifications that come from many of those careers and lifestyles. No one career or lifestyle is better than the other, but you should understand what to expect from your choices or lack of making choices.

For example, some of the questions you should ask yourself include: Can I achieve the lifestyle that I want on a teacher's salary? Do I value helping others more than monetary compensation? Can I provide for a family and myself by earning a minimum wage? Will I enjoy and embrace the sacrifices it takes to earn a six-figure annual income? Will I be committed to get the proper education that is required to master a certain profession?

You should ask and answer, how much does it cost to provide food, shelter (rent or a mortgage), transportation, education, and health care for myself and or my family? What does it cost to go on a vacation every year? Will I live on a two-family income? If so and if not, will I earn enough to live according to my desired standard of living?

Conclusion
Explore living costs, housing (rent or mortgage), food, education, health insurance, travel, auto payments/maintenance/insurance, utilities, child care costs and other expenses. Evaluate the income and the reward from your career choices. Your choices may change over time but you should understand the consequences of the path you choose.

Quotes
Love what you do and it will not be called work.
Jim Rohn

You are free to choose, but you are not free from the consequences of your choice.
Unknown

Don't pick a job with a great vacation package; pick one that doesn't need escaping from.
Unknown

Personal Experience
Picking a career can be difficult and create a lot of uncertainty. I spent a lot of time trying to determine what career path to choose. Back then we did not have Google. I visited the library many times researching various careers and job opportunities, often leaving quite frustrated. From teaching seeing eye dogs to becoming a pilot (I found out that due to my poor vision I would not be eligible to fly for the airlines as they required 20/20 vision), I continued to search only to remain uncertain.

I remember one cold winter night when I was helping my father replace the starter on my mother's car. The car was in the street at the curb. My father was lying on his back with a hunting outfit on to keep him warm as he twisted and turned the wrenches and ratchets. I was holding the light so he could see as he worked, and I ran to go get whatever tool he requested next (the gopher).

My father was quite talented. He knew how to fix a car, build furniture, sew a suit and repair electronics. After serving in the Marine Corp for 10 years, my father started his second career as a carpenter and later became a construction manager. He constructed many buildings as small as a house and as large as a Ford Motor Company plant, which at the time was the largest building built in Michigan.

Although my father and I discussed my career possibilities, we both acknowledged that I was still confused as to what career I would pursue in college. My father had some great advice for me. He said that he did not think I would become a doctor, lawyer, engineer or scientist. Therefore, he recommended that I surround myself with experts and manage their talents in a way that would bring me better results than me attempting those talents myself.

My father explained that the owner of the company he worked for, William Weatherford, hired a CPA to manage his money; an architect to design his buildings; an engineer to design infrastructure such as water, sewer and roadways; and hired my father to be his construction manager. Mr. Weatherford also had a sales team, even though he was very good at selling himself.

I follow my father's advice and always seek those who have greater talents than I to do those things that require specific talents. By being a manager, I have been able to enjoy the teamwork that is required to reach great achievements with others. I picked the construction and development industry, but it could have been any other industry. There are many to choose from.

Recommended Book

Go Big! Make Your Shot Count in the Connected World
Cory Cotton

Income and Expense Summary

Below is a summary of four different levels of income:
- Choice A
- Choice B
- Choice C
- Choice D

Income Levels range from:
- Choice A, an unskilled laborer
- Choice B, minimum skilled laborer
- Choice C, a two to five-year professional with a college degree
- Choice D, a six to ten-year professional with a college degree

1. The first portion shows income along with estimated taxes leaving net pay per month. (1)

2. The net pay is an estimated typical expense for the four choices, A, B, C and D. These are only estimates and actual expenses will vary based on numerous factors, but they are shown to give you an idea of some of the costs that the average person encounters and the remaining funds available for items like vacations, childcare, additional education, travel and other such expenses.

3. Rent/mortgage payments estimated at 33 percent of net pay leaving the balance of net pay for remaining items. For example, in the case of

choice A, an unskilled laborer, the allowance is $400 per month. This might be for a studio or a shared living arrangement. As the income rises, a larger monthly payment is available for a larger or more expensive living arrangement.

4. Total expenses are an estimate of various expenses you will most likely incur during your lifetime.

5. Cash available per month for savings. The purpose of this exhibit is to show that based on your income you will first have to pay for rent, utilities, auto expense, insurance, food and other necessities before any discretionary income is available. Your income limits your ability to acquire a larger or nicer place to live or a newer or nicer automobile. Your income limits your lifestyle, and if you don't increase your income over time you will not be able to improve your standard of living.

For households with two incomes, add the two together because most likely you would be sharing many of the expenses, however some items would increase, such as having two cars, two phones, more food and when children arrive, childcare.

INCOME				
	Choice A	Choice B	Choice C	Choice D
	Unskilled Labor	Minimum Skilled	2-5 Year College Degree	Professional 6-10 Year
Hour	$ 8.50	$15.00	$24.00	$50.00
Week	$340	$600	$960	$2,000
Month	$1,462	$2,580	$4,128	$8,600
Year	$17,500	$30,900	$49,536	$103,200
Tax Rate	12%	14%	17%	21%
Estimated Taxes	$2,163	$4,173	$8,177	$21,967
Net Pay/Yr	$15,337	$26,727	$41,359	$81,233
Net Pay/Mo.	$1,278	$2,227	$3,446	$6,769

	EXPENSES			
	Choice A	Choice B	Choice C	Choice D
Rent/Mort. (33%)	$400	$764	$1158	$2234
Home Insurance	$0	$0	$75	$300
Real Estate Tax	$0	$0	$200	$375
Health Insurance	$50	$200	$230	$230
Utilities:				
Electric	$50	$100	$150	$200
Water/Sewer	$30	$50	$75	$75
Cell Phone	$30	$30	$40	$50
Cable TV	$35	$50	$50	$50
Internet	$50	$50	$50	$50
Auto:				
Payment	$100	$150	$200	$250
Gas	$100	$150	$200	$200
Maintenance	$50	$50	$50	$50
Insurance	$50	$50	$100	$100
Household Exp:				
Food	$273	$400	$500	$600
Cleaning	$10	$10	$30	$50
Health Access	$50	$50	$75	$100
Misc.	$1	$3	$100	$100
Travel	$0	$50	$100	$100
Education	$0	$50	$100	$100
Vacations	$0	$0	$0	$200
Child Care	$0	$0	$0	$660
TOTAL EXP	$1,278	$2,204	$3,383	$6,074
Cash Available per Monthly Savings	$0	$23	$63	$695

Career Choices

Top 10 best jobs in 2015

Dentist

Nurse Practitioner

Software Developer

Physician

Dental Hygienist

Physical Therapist

Computer Systems Analyst

Registered Nurse

Physician Assistant

Information Security Analyst

*See US News & World Report for top 100 best jobs in 2015.

Understanding Wages

The following schedules: were provided by the U. S. Bureau of Labor and Statistics (BLS) OES survey. The schedules show various types of jobs including their total employment, Median wage, low, high and wage difference. Variation of wages can be due to location, education, experience, performance as well as other factors.

Profession	Total Employed	Medium Wage	Lowest 10% Wage Earners	Highest 10% Wage Earners	Wage Difference
Actor Actress	59,200	$ 41,200	$ 18,700	$187,000	$ 16,900
Admin. Judge Hearing Officer	14,200	$88,000	$42,000	$157,000	$115,000
Air Traffic Controller	22,900	$122,400	$67,000	$172,000	$105,000
Athlete	11,500	$ 43,400	$ 20,200	$187,000	$167,000
Attorney	604,000	$115,000	$55,000	$187,000	$132,000
Chief Exec. Officer CEO	246,000	$173,300	$72,800	$187,000	$114,000
Commercial Pilot	38,200	$76,000	$36,000	$141,000	$106,000
Dentist	98,000	$149,500	$70,000	$187,000	$117,000
Economist	18700	$95,700	$50,500	$171,000	$120,000
Engineering Manager	179,300	$130,600	$83,800	$187,000	$103,600
Financial Service Sales Agent	316,400	$72,000	$32,200	$187,000	$155,000
General Manager	2,050,000	$97,300	$45,100	$187,000	$142,000
General Practitioner	125,000	$180,200	$72,000	$187,000	$115,000
Higher Education Admin.	131,000	$88,400	$50,200	$174,000	$123,000
Higher Education Teacher	1,522,000	$63,000	$29,000	$139,000	$110,000
Human Resource Manager	116,600	$102,800	$60,400	$184,000	$123,000
Judge and Magistrate	28,100	$115,200	$31,500	$179,000	$147,000
Petroleum Engineer	38,800	$13,000	$74,000	$187,000	$113,000
Pilot and Flight Engineer	76,000	$118,000	$65,000	$132,000	$122,000
Real Estate Agent/Broker	38,700	$57,400	$23,900	$179,000	$155,000
Sales Engineer	68,200	$96,300	$55,900	$160,000	$104,000

NOTES

Twelve
Eight Reasons for Self Development

The more a person grows physically, mentally and emotionally, and the more one learns about him or herself, the more they can help others. This makes their life more significant personally and more significant for those with whom he or she has relationships.

Eight reasons why self-development is so important:

1) It teaches you to acknowledge you have control of your life.
2) It teaches you to accept that life is tough and to be prepared.
3) It teaches you the importance of setting your goals.
4) It teaches you what you believe is what you will seek.
5) It teaches you to be positive and remove negative things from your life.
6) It teaches you to maintain positive self-esteem and build positive relationships.
7) It teaches you to become personally and financially independent.
8) It teaches you to live a balanced lifestyle.

Quotes
I used to say, if you will take care of me, I will take care of you: Now I say, I will take care of me for you, if you take care of you, for me.
Jim Rohn

If you improved only 1 percent every day then guess what? In 100 days you would be 100 percent better.
Unknown

Personal Experience
I believe one of the greatest gifts you can give to somebody is to introduce him or her to a personal development program. Once an individual is familiar with the $10 billion-personal development industry (U.S. alone), they will find unlimited resources to assist them in many ways to improve themselves. By improving personally, we help those around us.

One of the most satisfying things about life is when one accomplishes more than one thought one could and to help others achieve more than they ever thought they could. This creates self-confidence and self confidence and self-respect, something that is yours forever.

Recommended Books

Man's Search for Meaning
Viktor E. Frankl

The Prophet
Kahlil Gibran

NOTES

_____

_____

_____

_____

_____

_____

_____

_____

_____

_____

_____

_____

_____

_____

_____

_____

_____

_____

_____

_____

_____

Thirteen
Self-Development/Mentors

A sure way to get ahead and get more from your efforts is to have mentors in your life. Sometimes it is just helpful to bounce ideas off them. Sometimes, you may be coached through others' experiences. Do not ignore the benefits of learning from others.

Many great athletes reached their greatness when a certain coach and or mentor entered their lives. Most believe, Peyton Manning, David Beckham, Tiger Woods, Derek Jeter, LeBron James, Mohammad Ali and Michael Jordon (to name a few) may not have reached greatness without the teachings of their coaches and mentors David Cutcliffe, Sir Mirren Ferguson, Dru Joyce, Yogi Berra, Butch Harmon, Angelo Dundee and Phil Jackson who are all world-renowned mentors who have contributed to greatness.

Conclusion
Always have a mentor and/or a coach on your team. To win big without them is highly unlikely. Soon you will become one too.

Quotes
A good coach will make his players see what they can become rather than what they are.
Ara Parseghian

We make a living by what we get; we make a life by what we give.
Winston Churchill

A lot of people have gone farther than they thought they could because someone else thought they could.
Unknown

In learning you will teach and in teaching you will learn.
Phil Collins

Ask for help not because you're weak, but because you want to remain strong!
Les Brown

Personal Experience

Without the mentors in my life, I would still be working in the phosphate mines in Bartow, Florida alongside convicts at near minimum wage. When the summer ended my supervisor, Mr. Smith, took me to say goodbye to the plant manager, Mr. Wilcox. Mr. Smith said, "We're sad Mr. Mike will be leaving us; he is going back to college." Mr. Wilcox turned in his chair and said, "No we're not sad, Mr. Mike is moving on to get a different education. He has learned what he can from us, and now it's time he learns from others."

I learned how to appreciate a job, those I work with and my supervisors. Later in my career, many of my supervisors became my mentors. I learned that they would teach me things, and in return I realized the importance of making their lives better and easier. The more I improved their situation the more I received in return.

I have always tried to make proud those that gave me their time and support. Mr. Wilcox is no longer living, but if he was, I hope that he would be proud of me. Nobody wants to help others only to have it be a waste of their time. There are no guarantees, but you will get more help in life if you return positive results. That is just the way it works.

Recommended Books

Mentoring 101
John C. Maxwell

The Last Lecture
Randy Pausch, PhD.

NOTES

_____

_____

_____

_____

_____

Fourteen
Self-Development Books,
Videos and Seminars

There are many ways to improve one's self. Reading is the oldest, most frequently used way of learning and exploring unlimited subjects, both enjoyable and beneficial in a person's life. However, most people only read a book or two per year. Those that achieve a higher percentage of their goals, dreams and objectives read several books a year. Individuals who are within the top 10 percent of their profession often read as many as one book per month. Reading is a requirement to be a top performer.

Many popular personalities freely give their best advice. These same people and others live their lives teaching and sharing their experience. In today's quick moving world, it only takes a second to search Google or YouTube for motivational topics. There are thousands of soundtracks and videos conveying unlimited messages. If you listen and watch, these messages will provide you with an education that you will remember for a lifetime. By absorbing such information, you will see the results. Listening and watching can provide a great deal in a relatively short period of time.

Conclusion
If you want to be a high achiever, read as many publications as you can. Start with magazine articles, short stories and books written about subjects you enjoy and love. Try audio books to better utilize driving time and supplement your reading experience. Google or YouTube motivational speakers to find material about unlimited topics. Continue to expand the topics you read and learn about as a key to your self-development.

When walking, exercising or traveling, listen to ebooks of interest. When you can, start reading paperback or hard cover books that interest you. Start with books about subjects you enjoy, hobbies or books about your profession. Begin with just 15 to 30 minutes a day. You will naturally increase the time you spend reading as you experience joy and success. This will help you reach your goals and become one of the few who reach the top 10 percent in your field. The unlimited reading resources that are available will change your life.

Quotes
Reading is to the mind what exercise is to the body.
Sir Richard Steel

The man who does not read good books has no advantage over the man who can't read.
Mark Twain

The more you read the more things you will know. The more you learn the more places you will go.
Dr. Seuss

Books allow you to simulate the future without actually having to do all the trials and error yourself. I read a lot.
Tai Lopez

Ordinary people have big TVs; extraordinary people have big libraries.
Robin Sharma

Personal Experience
I have enjoyed reading self-help books from the age of 16. They have allowed me to learn how I can improve myself in ways that I didn't know about prior to reading about these ideas. I never excelled in any particular discipline such as medicine, science, math, computers, acting, etc. Learning to improve myself assisted me in taking advantage of opportunities and therefore advance beyond others at work and in my profession. This occurred even when others may have been better educated, with more knowledge, talent and experience than me. This will work for you too.

Today there are more tools available to assist you regarding self improvement. I relied mostly on tape cassettes. You have better technology, including iPads, smart phones, personal computers, tablets, and more to provide instant online access to eBooks, YouTube videos, speeches, articles, daily messages from personal coaches, book clubs, and various other publications both in print, audio and video.

Recommended Book

Think and Grow Rich
Napoleon Hill

Recommended Videos
(Select one or more videos below to get started.)

Ten Rules for Success on YouTube by Evan Carmichael

Denzel Washington's Top Ten Rules for Success

Muhammad Ali's Top Ten Rules for Success

Tony Robbins' Top Ten Rules for Success

Rich Man Poor Man Top Ten Rules for Success

Work Hard Top Ten Rules for Success

Eric Thomas' Ten Rules for Success

Les Brown's Ten Rules for Success

Dan Pena's Ten Rules for Success

Mark Zuckerberg's Ten Rules for Success

Kevin O'Leary's Ten Rules for Success

Lee, Cardon, Paul Greatness Motivation Ten Rules for Success

Kobe Bryant's Ten Rules for Success

Jobs, Gardner, Trump, Ferriss Ten Rules for Success

Steve Wozniak's Ten Rules for Success

Michael Jordon's Ten Rules for Success

Larry Pag's Ten Rules for Success

Wayne Dyer's Ten Rules for Success

Richard Branson's Ten Rules for Success

Donald Trump's Ten Rules for Success

Warren Buffett's Ten Rules for Success

Napoleon Hill's Ten Rules for Success

Eminem's Ten Rules for Success

Jim Rohn's Ten Rules for Success

Bezos' Ten Rules for Success

Ma's Ten Rules for Success

Cuban's Ten Rules for Success

Stallone's Ten Rules for Success

NOTES

_____
_____
_____
_____
_____
_____
_____
_____
_____
_____

Fifteen
Personality

Stop and ask yourself when the last time was that you analyzed your own personality. Ask yourself, "do I like myself? Do people like me?" Most people do not realize that they have some input as to how their personality develops throughout their lives. It is our responsibility to learn and manage our personality. Failure to do so leaves one on the sideline or in the back of a crowd. It can be as easy as being a good listener, smiling, having a good handshake, speaking positively, or just being yourself and not trying to be somebody you are not.

Conclusion

Take charge of your personality. If you do not like yourself, perhaps others do not either. You have the opportunity to improve your likability, and if you do it will bring you much in return. There are as many different personalities as there are rocks in a pond. Some get along with others better than others do. There is no perfect personality, after all that is what makes us all different. However, by recognizing that we have control of how we behave with and around others, we can develop habits that promote positive relationships. It takes time, energy and the desire to do so.

Quotes

People who like you will most likely help you. Those that don't will often create road blocks. In life we need all the help we can get.
Author

Two things define your personality: the way you manage things when you have nothing and the way you behave when you have everything.
Unknown

Someone's opinion of you doesn't have to become your reality!
Les Brown

Personal Experience

Throughout my real estate development career I have consciously tried to get people to like me, even if I did not care for them. I have learned that it is much better to try to get people to like you than to stand back and let them become your enemy. Without making the effort, things can get out of hand. When I have ignored a relationship, it usually deteriorated. Of course, I have fallen short on many occasions, but I continue to try. You cannot always win people over, but if you try, you have the opportunity to make them want to help you rather than harm you.

Recommended Books

How to Win Friends and Influence People
Dale Carnegie

I'm OK, You're OK
Thomas H. Harris M.D.

NOTES

_____

_____

_____

_____

_____

_____

_____

_____

_____

_____

_____

_____

_____

_____

_____

_____

Sixteen
Being Positive

Being positive is perhaps the most important part of a person's life. Being positive starts with what you are thinking. It is reflected in what you say and in your actions. Those that control their thoughts usually have positive things to say. Those who speak in a positive manner more often than not take a positive approach to life. Positive people find themselves on the right side of many issues. People who act positively are better liked, listened to by more people, and influence others at a greater rate. Positive people live a more enjoyable life.

Conclusion
Think, speak and act in more positive ways and you will have more friends, impact more people and get more from your efforts than if you think, speak and act negatively.

Quotes
The mind is everything. What you think, you become.
Buddha

Whether you think you can or you think you can't, you're right!
Henry Ford

Worrying does not empty tomorrow of its troubles. It empties today of its strength.
Unknown

Once you replace negative thoughts with positive ones, you'll start having positive results.
Willie Nelson

You cannot have a positive life and a negative mind.
Joyce Meyer

Personal Experience
Al Johns, president and founder of Punta Gorda Isles, Inc., told me I was the most tenacious and positive person he had met during his 40 years in business. I had to look up what tenacious meant, but I knew what he

meant by positive. Being positive will overcome practically everything, impress most everyone and help you keep a smile on your face most of the time.

I, like many people, am not always in a positive state of mind. Many influences can quickly turn one toward negativity, particularly in personal matters when dealing with those who are close to you and your loved ones. Unfortunately, this is sometimes difficult to do, but in personal relationships we should be the most positive of all. I am making an effort to do so, but I recognize that I have a ways to go.

Recommended Book

The Power of Positive Thinking
Norman Vincent Peale

NOTES

_____

_____

_____

_____

_____

_____

_____

_____

_____

_____

_____

_____

_____

_____

_____

Seventeen
Perseverance

Very few things accomplish more than pure perseverance. When others give up, those who persevere ultimately win. Education is a necessity, but many highly educated people find themselves short of their goals. Brilliance is a remarkable trait, but many brilliant people also fall short of their goals. Perseverance, once understood and utilized, elevates a person beyond their goals, prevents failures and insures rewards.

Conclusion
When in doubt, when in trouble, when you have not yet won, keep persevering and in time you will be rewarded for your efforts.

Quotes
I'm convinced that half of what separates the successful entrepreneurs from the non-successful ones is pure perseverance.
Steve Jobs

I am not afraid of storms, for I am learning how to sail my ship.
Louisa May Alcott

Through perseverance many people win success out of what seemed destined to be certain failure.
Benjamin Disraeli

Personal Experience
I am not sure how I learned to be persistent. Perhaps my father taught me to finish what I started. My first job out of college was working as an assistant construction superintendent. My supervisor, Jack Brenner, told me that the last 10 percent of constructing a building was 90 percent of the work. That is how he allocated my bonuses; I received my bonuses at the finish line.

Later in my career, I was assigned to the red team. There was a green team and a red team. The green team started construction projects. When they got behind schedule or stalled, the red team was called in to finish. This is where I learned the most and how to overcome challenges, obstacles and adversity. You will too.

Recommended Books

Rise and Grind
Eric Thomas

The Road Less Traveled
M. Scott Peck

NOTES

Eighteen
Patience

Patience is a personality trait that you either are born with, or it can be learned over time. Sometimes patience will provide rewards that will not come in any other way. In some situations timing is critical and only patience will improve your timing. Forcing a round stick into a square hole often creates more confusion and conflict. Waiting until you find the round hole for a round pole often accomplishes more.

Conclusion
When in doubt or in the absence of being sure, be patient and perhaps what you're looking for will show up.

Quote
When things don't happen right away just remember it takes six months to build a Rolls Royce and 13 hours to build a Toyota.
Unknown

Two things define you - your patience when you have nothing and your attitude when you have everything.
Unknown

Personal Experience
Dan Boone, one of my lawyers for more than 30 years, always advised, "When you're not sure what to do, don't do anything. It may come to you and when it does, take the proper action." This has proved to be the greatest advice many times over.

My son, Michael, says, "Dad, you have two speeds. One is too slow and one is too fast." I am working on finding the right speed.

Recommended Book

The Power of Intention
Wayne Dyer

NOTES

Nineteen
Life Is Tough

Many people are surprised and experience extreme difficulty when they encounter life's challenges - tough times. Life seems easy for some and lucky for others until the unexpected occurs. Tough times may be an illness, death of a friend or relative, divorce or financial setbacks. People who realize that bad things will happen prepare and find better transitions through these tough circumstances.

Not to wish it on anyone, but statistics prove that tough times will come to all. By acknowledging it and planning you will be better prepared for the tough times.

Conclusion
Recognize that when, not if, tough times will arrive in your life. Be assured that there will be peace of mind and opportunity again once you have moved past the difficulty. Prepare for the unexpected. Be aware that you will overcome by utilizing the strengths that you have developed as you prepared for tough times.

Quotes
We see men who have accumulated great fortunes, but we often recognize only their triumph, overlooking the temporary defeats, which they had to surmount before arriving.
Napoleon Hill, from Think and Grow Rich

When you get knocked down, be sure to fall on your back, because when you can look up, you can get up!
Les Brown

Life is not a problem to be solved, but a reality to be experienced."
Soren Kierkegaard

Personal Experience
Several economic downturns, including those in 1982, 1992 and 2008 all created major financial and personal setbacks for myself and for many others. During each downturn, I had to regroup, in both my personal relationships and my corporate life.

Although I had prepared for financial setbacks, I had not completed the tasks adequately. For example, I hired an estate planner (lawyer) to design a family trust, but never fully implemented the plan. Like many things in life, we often put things off to do later. In the recession in 2008, this incompletion cost me considerable financial losses.

As for personal relationships, I have learned that sacrifice, acceptance, compromise and forgiveness are all necessary to be successful.

These setbacks are part of life and you learn that they can beat you if you let them. Or you can pick yourself up and move forward to become better for it. In the end, you will judge yourself and others will judge you based on how you recover from these life experiences and where they take you.

Recommended book

I Can Do It
Louise Hay

NOTES

_____

_____

_____

_____

_____

_____

_____

_____

_____

_____

_____

_____

_____

Twenty
Fear

Fear, say some, is a disease. It ruins lives. Others see fear as something you overcome. Once you face something that you fear and overcome it, you realize that you need not fear it any longer. By overcoming one fear, you can see that you can overcome other fears. As in all learned experiences, practice improves positive outcomes. By using your accomplishments to address your fears you can avoid future fear.

Conclusion
Fear can be overcome, and you can learn from things that you once feared or found troubling.

Quotes
Fear stands for false evidence that appears real.
Les Brown

The cave you fear to enter holds the treasure you see.
Joseph Campbell

I fear not the man who has practiced 10,000 kicks once, but I fear the man who has practiced one kick 10,000 times.
Bruce Lee

A head full of fears has no space for dreams.
Unknown

F.E.A.R. has two meanings, Forget Everything and Run, Or Face Everything and Rise. The choice is yours.
Zig Ziglar

Personal Experience
Fortunately, I have experienced little fear with the exception of my fear that something could happen to my children. I have learned that you have to let go and let them live their lives just as my parents generation did.

As a young person and throughout my life, I certainly have had many narrow escapes; however, I have been fortunate to escape any major catastrophic events.

I have accepted that I need to face the possibilities of danger entering my children's lives. I tried to teach them to be aware, to have the character to do their best to stay safe, and to do the right things to avoid danger.

Recommended Book

How to Stop Worrying and Start Living
Dale Carnegie

NOTES

_____

_____

_____

_____

_____

_____

_____

_____

_____

_____

_____

_____

_____

_____

_____

_____

_____

_____

_____

_____

_____

Twenty One
Giving Is Receiving

There are many things to give and share. This includes your time, your love and your wealth. They are all important, and one is not more important than the other.

When you constantly give more time, love or wealth than you receive, your value increases. When your value increases, you receive more in return.

As you get more from your improved value, your accomplishments accumulate. Your ability to give more keeps the cycle moving in your favor.

Conclusion
Keep giving your time, love and wealth and you will achieve many accomplishments that come with your increased value.

Quotes
It's not what you leave to your children it's what you leave in them.
T. D. Jakes

From what we get, we can make a living; what we give, however, makes a life.
Arthur Ashe

Only by giving are you able to receive more than you already have.
Jim Rohn

Giving is not just about making a donation. It is about making a difference.
Kathy Calvin, CEO United Nations Foundation

Personal Experience
Throughout my personal and business life, I believed in donating to several non-profit organizations with the belief that in doing so I would receive much in return. At times, I felt it might have been somewhat selfish, but after experiencing the win-win outcome, I just kept doing it.

Although I have been more generous with money than my time, I have valued others who give their time as much as those of us who give with money.

After trying to keep a low profile in my charitable giving, I was encouraged by a professional manager of a large community foundation to allow my name to be placed on a building for which I was a major contributor. The explanation included that it is the duty of those who are blessed financially not only to give back to the community, but also to do it publicly to encourage others who are able to do the same. Over time, I have seen how this works and hope you have the opportunity to do the same.

Recommended Book

The Richest Man in Babylon
George S. Clason

NOTES

_____

_____

_____

_____

_____

_____

_____

_____

_____

_____

_____

_____

_____

_____

Twenty Two
Law of Attraction

All things in life, including the people around you, are affected by the law of attraction. The law of attraction is the name given to the maxim, "like attracts like," which in new thought philosophy is used to sum up the idea that by focusing on positive or negative thoughts a person brings positive or negative experiences into his or her life.

When you are nice, you attract nice people. When you are sad, you attract sad people. A bird of a feather flock together is a well-known saying that illustrates this correctly.

Successful people attract more success. Likewise, those that have little success often attract very little success. Even those who speak of illness are ill more often, and those who speak of good health are often most healthy.

Some believe in the law of attraction and benefit from their belief. Some do not and lose the advantage that comes to those who do!

Conclusion
You attract people and opportunities based upon how you think, how you are perceived by others and what you believe. So take the appropriate steps and you will experience life's best.

Quotes
See it in your mind and you can hold it in your hand.
Unknown

Science says, show me and I'll believe it. Faith says believe and I'll show you.
Unknown

Ask, believe, and receive. I attract to my life whatever I give my attention, energy and focus, whether positive or negative."
Michael Losier

You can't live a positive life with a negative mind.
Unknown

Celebrate as much as you can and complain as little as you can, and watch how much resources have already been aligned for you. It is right that you feel good. You're supposed to have fun!
Abraham Hicks

Personal Experience
Early in my career, I read that you become like those with whom you surround yourself. In addition, if you want to be successful you should associate with people who are successful.

Therefore, after I moved to Houston following graduation from college I joined the Houstonian. The Houstonian is a health club for the movers and shakers of the Houston business scene. It housed the American Productivity Center, an organization that promoted productivity among U.S. businesses. It was located on 25 acres in the heart of Houston's business center, adjacent to the west loop. It included a luxury hotel, tennis courts, outdoor jogging trail, and all the bells and whistles one would expect from a prominent hotel, spa and luxury resort.

Some members probably wondered why this young 23-year-old construction superintendent joined the club. I was not a health and exercise junkie like many of the members, but after spending $10,000 to join, I felt I was on my way to being rich and successful.

Although my workout ethic was not very impressive, I would show up every day at 6 a.m. to drink coffee, read the newspaper, meet and speak to some of the most successful people living in what was then a boom town. Often I would play tennis with men 20 and 30 years my senior. The stories and lessons I learned are priceless. I was doing just what I read in one of those self-improvement books, associating, learning and sharing time with those I wanted to be like.

Recommended Book

The Strangest Secret: For Succeeding in the World Today
Earl Nightingale

Twenty Three
Law of Abundance

Abundance means plenty of, or a very large quantity, of something. It is the innate tendency of nature to grow and become more. Life's force is to produce more and create more of everything. More trees, new plants, more fruit and new grass, new cars, new houses, new jobs. Abundance is everywhere in the universe, and it can also appear in your personal life if you let it in. People often associate it with money, but it can come in many forms - love, friendships, opportunities, fun, food, energy and spirituality.

Energy follows thought. When you constantly think of living life abundantly your energy creates positive actions directed toward what you seek. The world is full of abundance, and you only have to seek abundance to find it.

Conclusion
Seek abundance and let your energy take you there. Look around you and you will see it. It is up to you.

Quotes
When you are grateful, fear disappears and abundance appears.
Tony Robbins

True abundance isn't based on your net worth; it is based on your self worth.
Gabrielle Bernstein

Change the way you look at things and the things you look at will change.
Wayne W. Dyer

Personal Experience
I have been very fortunate from an early age. In high school, I cut a few lawns and sold a battery additive called VX-6. I did not make much money selling the product after paying the expenses. I shared my income with my friend Carl Kitzman because I didn't own a car and he drove me around to make my deliveries. The experience was well worth the effort.

In college, I worked for a real estate development firm managing small condominium projects, cutting the grass and cleaning cobwebs from the hallways. I also worked in the phosphate mine in Bartow, Florida and on construction sites as a laborer. I even helped my brother, Tim, paint houses at the University of Michigan one summer. This all prepared me to find employment after graduating from college in Florida in 1977.

I knew what I did not want to do for the rest of my life. Florida was in a recession, so I moved to Houston, Texas, which was experiencing an economic boom. That is where my real estate career got its start. It is a career that has provided me with much abundance in many areas of my life. I recently learned about the law of abundance and recognized why I have experienced it throughout my life. I hope you will too.

Recommended Book

Abundance and Law of Attraction - Down the Rabbit Hole
Sandra Collins

NOTES

Twenty Four
Body Language

It is not always what you say that people hear. Your body speaks loudly, both positively and negatively. What you wear speaks out. Look at others and see what they wear and how they act. You will see for yourself.

In today's world, being politically correct is considerably different than it has been in the past. Today, one may think it is politically correct to accept people for who they are, what they wear and how they act. To some extent, we all do accept each other for who we are.

However, that does not include dressing for failure, displaying rude facial expressions and generally being disrespectful for one's own amusement.

Conclusion
Use your body language and the clothes you wear to represent yourself in the most positive way. Re-read chapter Sixteen, Being Positive. It is worth it.

Quotes
Sixty percent of all human communication is non-verbal, body language. Thirty percent is your tone, so that means that 90 percent of what you're saying isn't coming from your mouth.
Mere Hitch

Smile even if you don't feel like it. Your body language helps determine your state of mind.
Gitte Falkenberg

The most important thing in communication is hearing what isn't said.
Peter Drucker

You can't act like flip flops and expect to be treated like Louboutins.
www.konselingkeluarga.com

Personal Experience
I'm saddened when I see young people trying to differentiate themselves by seeking attention by dressing, talking or acting in ways that most

people would consider disrespectful or negative.

Of course this has been going on for several generations. It is done in different ways by people in each generation, but it has been part of society since the beginning. My thoughts are only that somewhere along the line those that need or seek acceptance realize that what they wear, how they speak and how they act affects the reaction they receive from others.

The sooner you realize that what you get from others is often what you deliver to them the better you will be. If it does not work for you, then perhaps you are associating with the wrong people.

Recommended Book

When Life Sucks for Teens
Kirrilie Smout

NOTES

_____

_____

_____

_____

_____

_____

_____

_____

_____

_____

_____

_____

_____

_____

Twenty Five
Time Management

Time is the only thing in life that you cannot get back. Those that plan and use their time in a positive manner accomplish more of what they are seeking.

Sleeping is good for up to eight or nine hours a day, but sleeping longer only lets others enjoy what you are missing. Too much sleep has been found to be unhealthy.

Balance your time wisely and never deprive yourself of things you enjoy. Fun times may be used as rewards for the time you spend doing less desirable tasks that are mandatory.

Conclusion
Time is a precious resource, and because it is so valuable it needs to be a priority, not left to chance. Take charge of your time and use it as a precious commodity because it is.

Quotes
Your time is limited, so don't waste it living someone else's life. Do not be trapped by dogma ... Do not let other people's opinions drown out your own inner voice. And most importantly, have the courage to follow your heart and intuition.
Steve Jobs

The key is not to prioritize what's on your schedule, but to schedule your priorities.
Stephen Covey

The bad news is that time flies. The good news is you're the pilot.
Michael Altshuler

People often complain of lack of time, when the lack of direction is the real problem.
Zig Ziglar

Give me six hours to chop down a tree and I'll spend four hours sharpening the ax.
Abraham Lincoln

A year from now you will wish you had started today.
Karen Lamb

Saying that you don't have time to improve your thoughts and your life is like saying you don't have time to stop for gas because you are too busy driving. Eventually it will catch up with you.
Robin Sharma

Personal Experience

There are many good time management programs available, some of which I have taken. Unfortunately for me, I have never mastered efficient use of my time. Consequently, to achieve a certain task I have had to put more time into it than I would have if I had practiced better time management.

For example, I have had many 10 to 12-hour days, six to seven days a week, over the course of my lifetime. This would not be necessary if I would have managed my time more efficiently.

Take time to use your time wisely.

Recommended Books

Seven Habits of Highly Effective People
Steven R. Covey

The Power of Habit
Charles Duhigg

NOTES

_____

_____

_____

_____

_____

Twenty Six
Comedy

Nothing can be more beneficial than a good laugh. Comedy should be part of your daily medicine, as it will keep you in a positive mood. Laughing, smiling and sharing humor can increase your likability with others, something that can only help you.

Conclusion
Go to the comedy show often and share your experience with others. Read humorous books and publications. Laughter brings joy and releases negativity.

Quote
We spend the first 12 months of our children's lives teaching them to walk and talk and the next 12 months telling them to sit down and shut up.
Phyllis Diller

Personal Experience
On several occasions for our annual company party, we attended comedy shows. Not only was it a good laugh, but we also learned to laugh with one another rather than at one another.

Many nights when I find myself tossing and turning, I turn on the TV and search for stand-up comedy. After a few jokes I am ready to go back to sleep. Comedy works in personal relationships too. My wife and I invited her sister and our brother-in-law to go see "Fluffy" at my alma mater, University of South Florida, in the college's new concert hall. I did not really know who Fluffy was. Soon after he got started, he would stop in the middle of a joke and his loyal fans (practically all 5,000 people there) would finish the joke.

We were highly impressed and considered ourselves out of touch. We cannot wait to see Fluffy again; perhaps we will be able to finish some of his jokes with the other loyal fans.

By the way, his jokes were all in good taste and contained very little, if any, vulgarity. Being funny for two or more hours is tough, especially without adding color.

Recommended Book

Do You Talk Funny - 7 Comedy Habits to Become a Better Speaker
David Nihill

NOTES

Twenty Seven
Chanel My Rottweiler

Most everyone would love to have a pet at some point in their life. Of course, a dog is a man and woman's best friend. Cats are not far behind. It is a question of when and what kind is best for you. Many young people choose to have a pet without realizing the time and financial commitment that is required. Some acquire a pet and move away leaving the pet with their parents or siblings. Some experience financial challenges with owning a pet, especially when sickness or bad health is encountered.

Conclusion
Seriously consider if the time is right to acquire a pet and if your budget provides adequate cushion for the unknown.

Quote
A dog is the only thing on earth that loves you more than he loves himself.
Unknown

Personal Experience
My wife, Tammy, loves to shop. As we traveled to various getaways like Houston, Miami, New York, Washington D.C., Las Vegas, Portland and Boston we had to visit many stores to look at the designer handbags by Gucci, Louis Vuitton and Chanel. I could not see shelling out the money necessary to purchase such handbags, so we did not purchase one of these collector items.

Next, we were off to get a puppy that would eventually weigh 100 pounds. When considering a name, and going through all the famous designer names, states etc., I told Tammy to choose one of the designer names, like Chanel, because that would be the closest thing she would ever get to owning a $3,500 Chanel handbag. We told this story to our veterinarian at the first appointment and the vet replied, "I've got news for you, you will be spending a lot more on your new puppy than the $3,500 that handbag would have cost you, but you will receive a lot more joy with the puppy." She was right on both counts.

In addition, to the normal costs of owning a pet, our Rottweiler is blind in one eye as a result of an unknown trauma to her right eye. We attempted to correct her vision with surgery, but it failed. However, she is doing very well with just the sight in her left eye. To compensate, she utilizes her sense of smell much more than she did prior to her accident. This is just one of the many unanticipated expenses that could take place. By the way, I eventually broke down and bought Tammy a designer handbag!

Recommended Book

My Dog; The Paradox
Oatmeal Matthew Inman

NOTES

_____

_____

_____

_____

_____

_____

_____

_____

_____

_____

_____

_____

_____

_____

_____

_____

_____

_____

_____

_____

Twenty Eight
Trigger

Something occurs in a person's life that redirects their efforts, beliefs and/or actions. I refer to this as a trigger. Once you pull your trigger, you are on your way to successfully pursuing your purpose in life. With a purpose in life, many things fall into place. Occasionally, one will experience setbacks or difficulties, but with a purpose, one will always recover quickly.

Conclusion
Be alert and seek a trigger you can pull that will direct you toward finding your purpose in life. With a purpose, your days will be full of accomplishments and you will experience restful nights.

Quote
A writer, who waits for ideal conditions under which to work, will die without putting a word on paper.
E.B. White

Personal Experience
During a family vacation from Detroit to Miami when I was 16, I spent time at my Uncle Bill's home, in his library, in his 70th floor penthouse office, sailing on his 60-foot yacht and piloting his 17-foot Boston Whaler for a few days in the Florida Keys.

He shared some of his favorite books, *Think and Grow Rich* by Napoleon Hill and *How to Win Friends and Influence People* by Dale Carnegie. Uncle Bill shared his life story from being a sales representative at a major life insurance company to becoming the president of the company.

After experiencing the accomplishments and the lifestyle that Uncle Bill had achieved, I realized that I too could set and reach goals. My trigger was pulled and I proceeded to find my purpose in life. It was like fuel in my tank that propelled me forward. Thanks Uncle Bill!

Recommended Book

Life Without Limits
Nick Vujicic

NOTES

Twenty Nine
Circle Of Life

Four things create a "Circle of Life." Once you acknowledge and understand this, you can use this to move your life in a certain, positive direction.

They are potential, action, results and belief.

We start with potential. Everybody has potential. How much may be the question, but everyone has potential. Some may have more than others. The potential leads you to action. The more action you take, the more results you achieve. Then the more results you receive, the more belief you have in yourself. The more belief you have in yourself, the more potential you will see that you have.

Increased potential leads to greater action. Greater action leads to more results. More results lead to more beliefs. Thus your potential increases once again.

Why do successful people become more successful? Rich become richer. Healthy people become healthier. Conversely, poor or unhealthy people often see themselves as poor or unhealthy and remain so.

Conclusion
Get on the Circle of Life. Recognize you have potential, take action, get results, increase your belief in yourself and your potential will increase. It is like a circle.

Quote
Use the Circle of Life to roll toward your dreams and desires.
Author

Personal Experience:
Soon after moving to North Palm Beach after high school, I began playing tennis with Craig Johnson who later became my boss. He hired me to take care of his condominium projects and to keep him in shape playing tennis. He was six-foot-six and had an arm span of at least 12 feet. It was quite difficult to hit the tennis ball around him or to lob it over his head.

He would beat me three out of four times and say, "You have potential, but you need more action." He said if I had a little "more action" I would get more results. Then he said that when I believed that I could beat him, I probably would. He was right. I finally beat him regularly three out of four times. It is only fair to admit that he was at least 20 years my senior.

Recommended Book

Finish Strong: Amazing Stories of Courage and Inspiration
Dan Green

NOTES

Thirty
Fear of Failure And Fear of Success

Many people do not take a step toward their dreams because they have a fear of failure or even the fear of success. They may not understand that failing along the way actually brings one closer to one's dreams. All dreams are found behind attempts that fall short. The only failure would be to stop the day before you would have reached your dreams.

Some say you should just "fail all the way to success." By the way, you learn more from your setbacks than many of your successes.

Conclusion
Failure helps you become closer to what you're striving to succeed and no one has ever reached their successes without using failure to get there.

Quotes
It's not about money or connections. It is the willingness to out work and out learn everyone when it comes to your business. And if it fails, you learn from what happened and do a better job next time.
Mark Cuban, Addicted2success.com

Fail so you can reach what you're looking for.
Author

It's fine to celebrate success, but it is more important to heed the lessons of failure.
Unknown

Failure ends when effort stops.
John Wesley Brown

Most people fail in life not because they aim too high, but because they aim too low and hit, or don't aim at all!
Les Brown

Don't worry about failures. Worry about the chances you miss when you don't even try.
Jack Canfield

Personal Experience

At age 25, I had the fortune to read a book called *With No Fear of Failure*, by Tom J. Fatjo, Jr and Keith Miller. It provided support for the belief that if you pursue your dreams without fear, you are sure to overcome the obstacles that you will absolutely face.

Once you overcome certain challenges and setbacks, you learn that failure has its benefits. As you learn from your failures, you will have more successes because of them. Ultimately, there is no reason to fear failure.

Recommended Book

With No fear of Failure
Tom Fatjo, Jr. and Keith Miller

NOTES

_____

_____

_____

_____

_____

_____

_____

_____

_____

_____

_____

_____

_____

_____

_____

Thirty One
Spiritual Being

Many people live and die without taking or having the time to develop their spiritual being. Those that do develop as spiritual beings have an advantage, because your beliefs ultimately drive your actions. Peace through the good and through the bad times can be found with certain spiritual beliefs. It is up to the individual to find their ultimate spirituality. When found, all else seems less important, less intimidating. You will find that regardless of what occurs in your life, by having a healthy spiritual relationship, regardless of the challenges you go through, in the end you will be just fine. If you search for it, you will find it.

Conclusion
Keep your eyes open and be open minded. Your life deserves to reach the highest level of fulfillment. You will find this spiritually.

Quotes
When you are going through something hard and wonder where a "supreme being" is, remember the teacher is always quiet during the test.
Unknown

Have patience with all things, but, first of all with yourself.
Saint Francis de Sales

When you are at your lowest look to the highest.
Unknown

Personal Experience
During my life, I always thought I was a good person. However, as I have had time to think more about my spiritual beliefs, I realize that I failed to get the most out of a spiritual relationship. It is never too late, and I am now enjoying the peace that one can obtain from belief in a "supreme being" and his teachings. Most of us will experience some kind of spiritual relationship in our lives. Sometimes it is when we encounter danger, death, divorce or some life-changing event.

I am not sure it's worth waiting for something to occur before one finds a spiritual relationship. It is like other things in life; the more you put into it the more you get out of it. Why wait?

Recommended Book

Tim Tebow - Through My Eyes
Tim Tebow and Nathan Whitaker

NOTES

Thirty Two
Living in the Now

The past can help with the future and you have to plan. However, if you live and take care of each day, you soon wrap up a series of good days that can make a great lifetime. Wake up each day with a purpose and live each day as if you do not know if it is your last, because you do not. If you do, you will experience the best you can be and much more than you thought possible.

Living in the now eliminates past troubles from keeping you from moving forward. Living in the now keeps negative thoughts of the future from affecting your daily enjoyment and accomplishments.

Conclusion
Spend most of your time getting the most out of each day and less time on the past and less worrying about your future. You cannot change the past and to change the future, take care of each day.

Quotes
The past is behind us, learn from it. The future is ahead of us, prepare for it. The present is here, live it!
Thomas S. Monson

Life is 10 percent what happens to us and 90 percent how we react to it!
Unknown

Personal Experience
Shortly after my second divorce, an Italian friend of mine, Michael Benestante, gave me a book titled *Buddha Made Simple*. It is just my kind of book because it has large print, is double spaced and it is less than 200 pages long.

It is an easy, quick read. It taught me to breathe one breath at a time and to live one day at a time. Many days have gone by since I read the book, but they all were better days because I chose to read it. You might want to pick up a copy.

Recommended Books

Buddhism Made Simple
Clive Erricker

The Power of Now
Eckhart Tolle

NOTES

Thirty Three
Leadership

Leadership has its privileges and its sacrifices. Not all people are leaders or need to be. If you choose to be a leader, you have to constantly work on yourself, always help others to improve and be willing to forgo the credit.

Remember, you cannot be a leader if nobody follows you. You can get a lot more accomplished when those that follow become better and even wiser than you. Never hold them back and be willing to let them move on. This is the sign that you have contributed to them as they have to you. Others will see the benefits that you offer, and you will continue to attract future leaders.

Conclusion
Lead, follow or get out of the way. When you choose leadership, you have a responsibility to help make others better than yourself.

Quotes
Treat a man as he is and he will remain as he is. Treat a man as he can be and should be and he will become as he can and should be.
Ralph Waldo Emerson

If your actions inspire others to dream more, learn more, do more, you are a leader.
John Quincy Adams

Do not go where a path may lead, go instead where there is no path and leave a trail.
Ralph Waldo Emerson

Personal Experience
One may wonder what makes a leader. First, I suppose you have to want to be a leader. Second, you have to know how to follow. Third, you have to be willing to do the things you ask others to do. Finally, you have to earn the respect from others and convince them that you have their best interests in mind as you proceed in the direction you want them to go.

One year at a company annual meeting, I was speaking to more than 100 employees. The real estate market was good and business was good. We were building and selling a house a day. Our sales peaked at $100 million in one year, our best year in housing sales.

As I faced the group, I took a minute to look into each of their eyes. Upon making eye contact with so many I could not help but think, not only of the employees, but I quickly thought of their wives, husbands and children too.

I stood proud to be their president and honored that I had gained their loyalty and support. It was obvious that they were the company and I was just their leader.

Recommended Books

The 21 Irrefutable Laws of Leadership World Book
John C. Maxwell

Good To Great
Jim Collins

NOTES

_____

_____

_____

_____

_____

_____

_____

_____

_____

_____

_____

Thirty Four
Wisdom

Wisdom is something we all wish to have, but seldom do we find enough to satisfy our hunger, therefore we seek more. Wisdom is defined as the quality of having experience, knowledge and good judgment, the quality of being wise."

Fortunately, there is always more room to learn and to expand your experiences, increase your knowledge and improve your judgment. Your journey is never over; it just covers more area.

Conclusion
Seek to be wise, but realize there is always more wisdom available to improve your life. You never become too wise, and when you just sit still, you will slide backward.

Quotes
Knowledge comes from learning. Wisdom comes from living.
Anthony Douglas Williams

What the mind can conceive, it can achieve.
Napoleon Hill

Personal Experience
I have always aspired to become a wise person. I am not sure you know when you have become a wise person. If you do not know if you are a wise person, you must keep seeking it out. Each day I learn something and I wonder why I have not already learned that. Then I learn something else and tell myself that I am not as smart as I thought I was. There is always more to learn. This keeps things interesting.

Recommended Book

The Original Chicken Soup for the Soul
Jack Canfield, Mark Victor Hansen and Amy Newmark

NOTES

Thirty Five
College and Higher Education

In today's world, you cannot end your education after high school graduation. Whether it's college, trade school or some other area of learning, you must find an avenue to higher earnings and a path to find your passion and purpose in life. College and higher education can provide that path.

College may not be for everybody, but to not pursue a trade or further your education will leave you in a very uncompetitive position in a very competitive world. With that said, it does not take an Ivy League college or even a high-ranking college to get a good education. There are many reasonable paths to a great education and they include state colleges, two-year colleges and online programs. If necessary, working while taking classes is an option that may prove beneficial without incurring excessive student loans. It may take longer, but you will learn from working too!

Conclusion
Although schools with higher name recognition can bring opportunity, it is not where you go, it is who you become that counts.

Quotes
Education is the best provision for life's journey.
Aristotle

A college degree is not a sign that one is a finished product, but an indication a person is more prepared for life.
Reverend Edward A. Malloy

Personal Experience
My formal education started at Palm Beach Junior College (now Palm Beach State College). One year later after earning money while attending school I transferred to University of South Florida (USF), located in Tampa, Florida.

Although it is a much-improved University today, one would not have ranked it a top college category at the time I graduated in 1977.

However, many successful people have received their college educations from institutions like USF. I have met and worked with many who have graduated from the best of schools. I always felt positive that although I did not graduate from a top ranked school I took second place to no one. You do not have to either.

Recommended Book

Looking Beyond the Ivy League: Finding the College that's Right for You
Loren Pope

NOTES

Thirty Six
Belief System

Perhaps the most important concept that influences a person's life is his or her own individual beliefs. I call this your belief system. Believing that you can achieve a goal, objective or a dream is the first and necessary step to moving closer to it. Moving toward it is the point. If you believe you can, you will move toward it. You will make a small step that gets you closer. That is all you need to get started. Once you get a little closer, you will believe that you will get there. You will start to smell it. Then you will keep moving toward it until you achieve it.

Conclusion
First, form your belief systems. Let them take you places and they will work for you. Just say, "It is possible," and you are on your way!

Quotes
The only thing that stands between you and your dreams is the will to try and the belief that it is actually possible.
Les Brown

What you tell yourself every day will either lift you up or tear you down.
Unknown

Forget all the reasons why it won't work and remember the one reason why it will.
Unknown

Ability is what gives you the opportunity; belief is what gets you there.
Apollo

Personal Experience
My favorite example of how powerful beliefs can be is the story of Roger Bannister breaking the four-minute mile. I liked it so much; I told this story at a commencement speech I gave at State College of Florida to the class of 2005, 30 years after I graduated from college.

Mr. Bannister, in 1954, after years of other people trying to break the four-minute barrier, accomplished what others could not. A year after, several runners broke the barrier. Once it was believed that the barrier could be broken, many runners ran the mile in less than four minutes. In fact, today, many high school students can run a mile in less than four minutes. Once you believe in something, your energy will take you toward it and it will become a reality. Using your beliefs, you will experience great achievements. Remember, just say, "It is possible "and you are on your way!

Recommended Books

Don't Sweat the Small Stuff and It's All Small Stuff
Richard Carlson PhD.

Thinking Fast and Slow
Daniel Kahneman

NOTES

_____

_____

_____

_____

_____

_____

_____

_____

_____

_____

_____

_____

_____

_____

_____

_____

Thirty Seven
80-Inch String

The four years following high school can be the most important period of your life. However, it is a very small portion of your life. This is the time when most high school graduates choose to go to college, seek additional education, or move right into the work force. Do not make a quick decision.

Think of the average lifetime being 80 years, then think of a string that is 80 inches long. Now take the first 18 inches or the first 18 years of your life and put two fingers from your left hand at the 18-inch line. Now take your right hand and two fingers and put them four inches or four years to the right at the 22-inch mark. Now, look at what is to the left of your left hand and look at what is to the right of your right hand. On the right, the string represents 58 inches or years left in the average person's life after four years following high school. The four inches between your hands, which represents the four years in college may be the most influential, directional, most critical years of your life. This will determine your direction for what will be 73 percent of your remaining life.

This time should be absolutely one of the best times of your life. After all, most people following this four-year period will be working for the majority of their remaining lives. This is the point, after high school, when you should explore the many career opportunities available to you. More importantly, you should seek your purpose in life. With a purpose you will not be working for your remaining lifetime, you will be enjoying each day of your life pursuing your dreams, your rewards and ultimately creating your legacy.

Conclusion
Enjoy, but take your tasks seriously for the four years after high school. It will determine the direction your life takes.

Quote
The value of a college education is not the learning of many facts, but the training of the mind to think.
Albert Einstein

Personal Experience

My time in college flew by as it does for most students. The last year seemed to drag on, but the few short college years were followed by many working years. I would encourage all students to enjoy the college life to its fullest.

Of course, that does not mean to engage in life threatening activities with long-term negative impacts on your future. Some mistakes will be made, but as long as they do not cause long-term harm and you learn from them, most likely you will be a better person for it.

Recommended Book

101 Secrets for Your Twenties
Paul Angone

NOTES

_____

_____

_____

_____

_____

_____

_____

_____

_____

_____

_____

_____

_____

_____

_____

_____

Thirty Eight
College Life Can Be Lonely

It is important to get involved with some social activities soon after you arrive at college. Many students become lonely due to the loss of their support group at home. Many do not realize how important new acquaintances are and may experience loneliness. All work and no play has its downside. Friends you go to college to be with may change paths or find other friends or get married. You may find yourself without the individuals with whom you thought you would share your new experiences. Add new friends and activities and expand your support group and your life experiences so that you can enjoy this period of your life in the most positive way possible.

Conclusion
Regardless of whom you think you will be with at college, make new friends so that you will not find yourself feeling alone. This will minimize your feeling of loss when you sometimes miss your family and friends back home. In addition, friends you make in college can remain friends throughout your life if you make the effort. Good friendships are important, not only as a resource to help one another, but because we tend to be similar to those we associate with.

Quote
I would rather walk with a friend in the dark than alone in the light.
Helen Keller

Personal Experience
My friend, Charlie, and I transferred from Palm Beach Junior College to USF and planned to live together at our new school. After the first semester, he moved back home and I found myself needing to make new friends and get new roommates.

I realized this happened to many other college kids. Unfortunately, I did not make the effort to join any clubs or organizations and consequently did not gain the friendships that are available to those who do.

Knowing what I know now, I should have spent more time participating in school events, clubs and activities developing friendships that could have been helpful in future years. I do not have to worry about my daughter, Mariah. She was very active in high school activities (basketball team, young Republicans Club. She was on the honor roll and carried a 4.86 GPA.) Mariah carried her habits to college. In her first year she is already involved with many activities, including the Republican Club and a pre-law fraternity.

Recommended Book

The Naked Roommate - A Year's Worth of Stuff You Might Run into in College
Harlan Cohen

NOTES

Thirty Nine
Know Your Surroundings

Most times, when you think of your surroundings you are thinking of your security. Of course, you should always be concerned for your safety and avoid being in the wrong place at the wrong time.

Just as security is important, it is important to know that the people and places you frequent can have a positive or negative influence on you and your ability to stay focused on your goals and objectives. Do your friends have the same morals, convictions and beliefs and are they driven to succeed? Are the places you hang out uplifting or do they break you down? You choose your surroundings, so do it with clarity.

Conclusion
Who you spend your time with and where you spend your time will have an important impact on your life.

Quotes
Your income will be the average of the five people you spend the most time with.
Jim Rohn

If you hang out with chickens, you're going to cluck and if you hang out with eagles, you're going to fly!
Dr. Steve Maraboli

Personal Experience
My Uncle Bob quit drinking alcohol when he was 45 years old. I asked him how he was able to stop drinking. He answered that he quit going anywhere where alcohol was available. I asked him what about after playing 18 holes of golf with friends, and he answered that his friends went to the 19th hole but he put his clubs and spikes in the trunk of his car and went home. Great advice!

Recommended Book

Choose Your Future
Les Brown

NOTES

Forty
Anger

Anger occurs in life when something goes wrong or when someone strikes out against us. Naturally, when this occurs we become angry with either ourselves or someone else. We cannot change that. What we can do is process the anger sooner rather than later. Being angry only hurts one's self. It rarely hurts the other person we have the strong feelings against. Therefore, the sooner we direct our energy toward something positive, the better we will feel. This will allow us to move toward a positive desired outcome.

Conclusion
Move the energy you generate from anger into positive efforts toward solutions or actions that create desired results.

Quotes
Anyone can become angry — that is easy. But to be angry with the right person, to the right degree, at the right time, for the right purpose, and in the right way — this is not easy.
Aristotle

Holding on to anger is like grasping a hot coal with the intent of throwing it at someone else: you are the one who gets burned.
Buddha

Personal Experience
I submitted a request for a site and development permit for a WalMart store planned on an existing commercial parcel. The planning commission denied my application after two years of seeking what was a lawful request that was completely within my property rights. Because it was improperly denied, I became quite angry. The chairman of the planning commission and the senior planner purposely delayed the approval for personal reasons. They successfully attempted to derail the WalMart Store by causing numerous delays.

The chairman had political aspirations, which included running for city council. The planner thought he would gain if the chairman was successful in his attempt to be elected from the "anti" WalMart, no-growth constituency. Even though we obtained approval 10 months later upon an appeal, the executives from WalMart decided not to purchase my property. This decision was affected by the deteriorating economy in 2008, as well as their frustration with the process.

After loosing several million dollars, I grew very angry and was not sure what I was going to do. In addition to this setback, we had more than 130 condominiums under construction that were scheduled to close upon completion of construction.

Because of the collapse of the economy, and in particular the real estate market, only a handful of the buyers closed on their condominiums. I was left with millions of dollars of finished condominiums that nobody wanted to purchase.

Even though the purchasers walked away from their 20-percent down payments, I did not have any anger toward them. In fact, I felt bad for those that closed because they had paid much more than the condominium units were now worth.

As for the chairman of the planning commission and the senior planner, my feelings were quite different. My anger toward their unlawful and selfish acts, which hurt far more people than just I, was hard to contain.

Shortly after my setback, the chairman lost the election for city council and the planner was let go from his job. I considered filing a multi-million-dollar lawsuit against the city for the unlawful acts of its employees and appointed representatives.

After much deliberation, I chose to direct my efforts toward saving my remaining assets and creating a new phase of my life, a life which would replace my anger with greater rewards than those I lost.

Recommended Book

The Cow in the Parking Lot - A Zen Approach to Overcoming Anger
Leonard Scheff and Susan Edmiston

Forty One
Words

Your words are your most powerful tools. They can be uplifting to you and to others. Likewise, words can be very hurtful to others, and self-damaging. Stop and think before you say things or be willing to take the consequences once spoken. Words seldom can be taken back. Once the door is opened and harsh or unkind words are spoken, they remain there forever.

Start each day with positive words. Listen to positive audio messages. What you hear and say when you first awaken in the morning will set the stage for your day. Improve your vocabulary so that you can be an effective communicator. Remember too that silence can be powerful as well.

The most powerful word is YES. If you become a YES person, you will achieve many successes. It is true also with the NO word. If you become a NO person, you will encounter many roadblocks.

Conclusion
Consistently improve your vocabulary. Think before you speak and you will improve your chances of getting your point across. Recognize that when you stop speaking you may communicate by being silent. Always say YES and proceed to make it happen.

Quotes
Be careful with your words, once they are said, they can only be forgiven, not forgotten.
Unknown

Take advantage of every opportunity to practice your communication skills so that when important occasions arise, you will have the gift, the style, the sharpness, the clarity, and the emotions to affect other people.
Jim Rohn

Personal Experience
Words have always intrigued me. I remember taking a vocabulary class in college. My friend, Steve Stortor, was slightly older than I was and he was studying physiology.

Steve had a great vocabulary. His father was a physiatrist. Steve got A's and I got a C's. Reflecting back, it is clear that I would have been well served to do better in vocabulary class and to continue to improve my word usage.

Unfortunately, when I worked in construction as a laborer, I developed a bad habit of using fowl words. I would release tension by shouting a few three and four-letter words. It worked, but I never got rid of the bad habit.

Using the right words can be a powerful, persuasive tool in communicating. Reading is a terrific way to expand one's vocabulary. I hope you do better than I did in college in your vocabulary class.

Recommended Book

Word Power Made Easy
Norman Lewis

NOTES

Forty Two
Manners and Respect

There are some basic manners that have fallen to the wayside in recent years. Parents, including me, hesitate to pester our children with what appears to be such little things, sometimes things that even seem petty. If one of our children loses a job opportunity because parents did not have the perseverance or tough love to teach them good manners, we might feel like failures.

Therefore, I recommend the following:

Do not use your cell phone (texting) constantly when visiting with others. It is rude. Use forks, spoons, knives, and not your fingers when eating. Chew with your mouth closed. Do not wear a hat when eating at the dinner table. Look people in the eyes when communicating. Use proper English. "Huh" is not a word. Respect others' property. Respect others by always saying "thank you" when someone goes out of their way to help or does anything nice for you. Do not text while driving. Dire consequences occur when texting and driving. Be on time or early to appointments. Keep your commitments. Spend some time with the older generation, especially your grandma and grandpa.

Respect will make up for having less talent. Respect will get you a second chance. Respect is something we all ask from others, and we only deserve respect if we deliver it first.

Conclusion
Be respectful by having good manners. By being considerate of others you will receive much in return. Likewise, failure to do so will certainly have negative consequences perhaps in the worst of circumstances.

Quotes
Be more concerned with your character than your reputation, because your character is what you really are, while your reputation is merely what others think you are.
John Wooden, Coach

Respect is earned. Honesty is appreciated. Trust is gained. Loyalty is returned.
Unknown

Seek respect, not attention. It lasts longer.
Unknown

One of the greatest gifts you can give to anyone is the gift of your attention.
Jim Rohn

Personal Experience

Having dinner with a combination of any of our eight children (18 to 33 years of age) and or their friends is a wonderful experience that we often enjoy. However, at times, this is where I experience some need for improvement regarding good manners and respect. We all need to recognize the importance of proper manners and respect. Proper manners and respect are necessary to get what you want from others in life. It can go along way.

A long time loyal employee, Marc Smith, is from Lubbock, Texas and has worked with me more than 27 years. There are two things about Marc. He has never missed a day's work and he always says, "Yes sir and Yes ma'am."

Even after a customer would inform him he didn't have to say "Yes sir" and "Yes ma'am," he would continue to respond in that way. Marc Smith is the best example of being consistently respectful of others, and therefore everyone he deals with goes away with a positive experience. Even when he has to tell them something they do not like, customers always remember Marc as the person with the best manners. It costs Marc very little to be this way, and he receives a lot of respect in return.

Recommended Book

Mind Your Manners: An Etiquette Guide for Youth and Young Adults
Edwardlene Fleeks Willis, PhD.

Forty Three
Peace of Mind

In this competitive and complicated world, it is important to occasionally stop and take a breath, then analyze where you are and who you spend your time with. Challenges, setbacks and difficult relationships will be part of your life. How we deal with them is most important. To combat stress, peace of mind is critical.

A good night's sleep, exercise, meditation, prayer and positive conversations with friends and family will add to your peace of mind.

Stay away from people who are needy. They drag you down. Enabling them will not help them. They need to take responsibility for their lives, just like you. Until then, they will only hurt you and themselves. Do them a favor and let them know that you seek to surround yourself with positive people and when he or she becomes positive to give you a call. Maybe they will.

Conclusion
Spend time relaxing. Look around you and see if you like your surroundings. Find peace of mind.

Quote
Be selective in your battles, many times peace of mind is better than being right.
Unknown

Someone else's action should not determine your response.
Dalai Lama

Personal Experience
Often, when I get upset or mad at someone, particularly a customer, I have a standard operating procedure (SOP). All of my assistants and close employees know what it is. At the point when I want to vent, I write a long detailed letter or email. Once complete, I read it and perhaps share it with those who know the circumstances. Once read, I throw it out without mailing or sending it. I feel much better, and most of the time the issues resolve themselves.

I learned this SOP after making the mistake of sending out similar letters only to cause more frustration and more damage. The procedure now leaves me with peace of mind.

Recommended Book

As a Man Thinketh
James Allen

NOTES

Forty Four
Personal Philosophy

Everyone has his or her own personal philosophy. Some people may not know that they do, but they do. This is why some people have little direction and why others have lots of ambition, drive and know what they want. Everyone develops their own personal philosophy through their life experiences, those they associate with and things they read and listen too.

Conclusion
Develop your own philosophy by making the right choices. Select with care those with whom you associate. Seek positive experiences that build personal beliefs that provide energy for success in all areas of your life.

Quote
Formal education will make you a living: self education will make you a fortune.
Jim Rohn

Personal experience
Like others, my philosophy has developed over the years and has changed with my life experiences. Fortunately, I have learned and believe that I alone have (as we all do) a major effect on my life and I must accept accountability for it. This does not mean that it is or will be any better than anyone else's will or that it is or will be without imperfection. What it does mean is that I can change certain things if I choose to and I can accept those things I cannot change.

Recommended Book

My Philosophy for Successful Living
Jim Rohn

Forty Five
Taxes

Everybody has heard the saying that death and taxes are the only two things in life that are for certain. There are various taxes a person encounters during their lifetime.

The major taxes are
1) Federal Income Tax
2) Social Security/Medicare Tax
3) State Income Tax (some states)
4) State, County and Local Sales Taxes
5) Real Estate Taxes
6) Use and other minor taxes.

A brief summary: (Note: this is just a brief summary and actual rates will vary based on rules, regulations and adjustments.)

1) Federal income tax (taxes on personal earnings from 10% - 39.6% based on earnings, the more you make the larger the tax rate.) These funds are collected by the government and are used to pay for National Defense, (25%), Health Care (22%), Income Security (17%), interest on government loans (8%), Veteran's Benefits (4.5%), Education and Job Training (3.3%)., Law Enforcement and Immigration (2%), Natural Resources, Energy, and Environment (2%), International Affairs (1.7%), Science, Space and Technology (1%).

2) Social Security/ Medicare tax rate for employee is 6.2% on the maximum of $118,000 of earnings and the same (6.2%) for the employer. A self-employed person pays a rate of 12.4 %.

3) Some states have a State Income Tax with rates from 0 to 11%. (There is no state tax in Alaska, Florida, Nevada, South Dakota, Texas, Washington and Wyoming). State income tax is in addition to federal taxes. Some states use other means of taxation to collect funds for costs incurred by States such as sales taxes. States use taxes to run state governments, including education, health care, transportation, correction facilities, low income assistance, police, parks, economic development, and health benefits to public employees, etc.

4) State, County and Local Sales Taxes range from a high of 9.45% in Tennessee to a low in Alaska of 1.76%. Five states don't have state sales taxes. Florida has a tax rate of 6%, plus additional local and county rates. For example, Sarasota County total rate is 7%. (You generally do not pay sales taxes on non-prepared food and medicine.) An additional resort tax and or bed tax is charged on lodging. For example, in Sarasota County you pay 5% on any rental of less than 6 months, which brings the total tax on a hotel room to 12%.

5) Real estate taxes are paid annually on property you own less a homestead deduction ($25,000/person in Florida) for your personal residence. For a residence with a taxable value of $200,000 the typical tax rate of $17.40 $1000 of value (City of Venice and Sarasota County) would be $3,480 per year. A person with a residence with a taxable net value of $1,000,000 would be $17,400 per year.

6) Death Taxes (estate taxes) top rates are 40% over $5,430.000 per person in 2015.

7) There are numerous other taxes, including building permit tax, commercial drivers license tax, cigarette tax, corporate income tax, dog license tax, excise tax, fishing license tax, food license tax, fuel permit tax, gasoline tax (42 cents per gallon), gross receipts tax, any many other "use taxes."

Our income tax system is based on a progressive tax, meaning higher rates for higher income earners ... these rates are offset by various deductions. Most people agree our system is too complicated and needs overhauling.

"In 1980, the bottom 90% of taxpayers paid 50.72% of income taxes. In 2011 (the most recent year the data is available), the bottom 90% paid 31.74% of the taxes. On the flip side, the top 1% paid 19.05% of taxes in 1980 and now pays 35.06% of taxes."
The top 50% of the income earners paid 97% of all taxes in 2011. The top 1% pays more federal income taxes than the bottom 90%.
Source: Tax Foundation.

Conclusion

Taxes are collected on just about everything to pay for all the governmental programs, benefits, entitlements and principle and interest payments on our national debt. Taxes may vary over time in rate and items taxed or exempted, based on governmental policy in place during Republican and or Democratic administrations and or control of the United States Congress and Senate.

Quote

For a nation to try to tax itself into prosperity is like a man standing in a bucket and trying to lift himself up by the handle.
Winston Churchill

Personal Experiences

Once understood, most people do not object to paying their fair share of taxes. Higher wage earners that I know do not mind paying more taxes than persons with lower incomes. However, a big concern is that taxes should be spent wisely and that the system should not have incentives for taxpayers that create dependency on government programs.

There is no worse place to be than to be restricted to a limited income or limited personal growth.

Recommended Book

Taxes For Dummies
Eric Tyson and David J Siverman

NOTES

_____

_____

_____

_____

_____

_____

_____

Forty Six
Setting Goals

Setting goals addresses the future. Your past has great value, but should never be allowed to cause you burden or hold you from moving forward. Some people face their future with apprehension, but you should face the future with positive anticipation. Your future should be designed by you. For example, you should decide what skills you want to learn, what income you want to earn, where you want to live, what habits you want to develop, what kind of friends you want to have, where you want to travel, what kind of life you want to live and what legacy you want to leave.

You have to write your goals down if you want to achieve them. Keeping old lists and making new lists is very important. The probability of achievement increases each time you write it down. Hanging them up on the mirror, on the refrigerator, on the front door, in your car, in your office will improve the likelihood that you will stay focused and hit your target. Try it.

Checking on your goals is required so that you will know if you are on track or if you are off course. Setting goals is like setting your sail on a sailboat. It sends you in the direction you intend to go. In a sailboat, you have to adjust your sails as the wind blows. If you do, you will arrive at your intended destination. If you do not, you will not. That is why writing down goals works.

Conclusion
Those that write down their goals, check on their progress often, and change course when needed will reach the desired destination.

Quotes
You set goals for what it makes of you if you achieve them, not for what you get from them.
Unknown

Don't wish for a better wind to blow you in the right direction but work on yourself to be better.
Jim Rohn

Commit yourself first and then find the how!
Unknown

You have to be willing to do things today others won't do in order to have things tomorrow others won't have.
Les Brown

Personal Experience
After my trip to Florida at age 16 years, I knew I did not want to live in Detroit, Michigan for my entire life. The winters were long and cold. My dream was to live on a canal in Florida, to own a boat and go fishing often. My parents moved to Florida after my last year in high school.

After enjoying the summer working as a laborer in the construction field, I learned two things. I did not want to go back to Detroit Michigan and I did not want to be a laborer in the construction field.

I was under no misconception. I understood it would take substantial earnings to enjoy the life style I desired. So at a young age, my first substantial goal was in place, but how I would achieve it was yet to be determined. Having a goal is the first step. You do not have to know how you will achieve it. That comes next.

Recommended Book

Goals! - How to get Everything You Want - Faster Than You Ever Thought Possible
Brian Tracy

NOTES

_____

_____

_____

_____

_____

_____

_____

Forty Seven
Financial And Personal Independence

Did you know that 76% of Americans live paycheck to paycheck? Did you ever ask why?

To become financially and personally independent you have to have the ability to live from your own personal income and from your own individual resources. Some people have concerns when people discuss money, wealth or becoming rich. I believe every person's heritage is to be financially and personally independent.

First, one would say you have to make enough money to pay your living expenses. Correct, but to be financially independent means that the assets you accumulate and the income you generate from investments earn you sufficient funds to support your living expenses.

To illustrate, there are two philosophies about spending, one of the poor and one of the rich. The poor usually spend their money and invest the rest. The rich invest their money and spend the rest.

A good habit to develop (as suggested by Jim Rohn) is to plan your spending. First, contribute 10 percent of what you earn to charity, a church, the poor or a worthy project. (You can decide the amount and start small then increase the amount.) Nothing teaches character more than generosity. By being generous, you will receive much in return and it will motivate you to earn more. It's the state of mind that drives you to earn. The drive to earn more money in order to purchase things does not have the same force. If you do not believe this, think about why rich people and other successful people keep working and keep making money. It's not because they need more food or a new car. It is because they enjoy it.

The second 10 percent (or what you decide) should be spent toward active capital. Active capital is from profits. Profits are better than wages because there is no limitation on profits like there is on wages. An example of a profit is purchasing something used, making it better and selling it for more than you paid for it. It can be a bike for a teenager, a car for a young adult or a rental house for a couple starting out.

The third 10 percent (or what you decide) is put toward passive capital such as stocks, bonds, interest from loans, etc. Investments from passive capital grow over time because they compound.. many people have become financially independent from passive capital.

The balance, 70 percent, is what you live on. This may seem impossible, but as you follow this structure, you will earn more money and over time find it to be extremely rewarding.

Conclusion
It has been said that a person can easily become personally financially independent over a 20-year period. If you're 18 that would make you 38. If you are 24 that would make you 44 years old. Even at 50, you would only be 70 years old when you become financially independent. Nowhere does it say it must take 20 years. It is your choice. It's how you spend your money and how much you decide to make. Everybody can become financially and personally independent.

Quote
It's not what you get when you earn your first million dollars it is who you become.
Jim Rohn

Personal Experience
Because of my early employment opportunities and those that followed, I was fortunate to earn above average earnings throughout my career. Being self-employed, I was able to adjust my income with the ups and downs of the economy. My long-term financial plan included owning income property that would produce a secondary income stream for my family and my retirement.

Although I lost most of my income properties during the recession of 2008, I have been able to reap the benefits of what has been retained. If I would have completed my family trust financial plan, I would have been able to retain a greater amount of the assets I had earned and the income that I had generated.

I would highly recommend that a financial asset protection plan be implemented at an early age and be maintained so that the assets earned cannot be lost to bad economies or other risks one may encounter throughout life. We live in a highly litigious society that requires asset protection by an experienced attorney prior to encountering any financial troubles.

Recommended Book

Rich Man Poor Man
Robert T. Kiyosaki with Sharon L. Lechter, CPA

NOTES

_____

_____

_____

_____

_____

_____

_____

_____

_____

_____

_____

_____

_____

_____

_____

_____

_____

_____

_____

_____

Forty Eight
Grateful

Gratitude strengthens relationships, improves health, reduces stress, and in general makes us happier people. Have you ever seen someone that said thanks who was mad at you?

If this is the case, then why do some people lack gratitude? Is it because they take things for granted? Is it because they did not earn what they received? Do they feel they are entitled?

Conclusion
Of course, there will always be those that are not grateful, however, those who are grateful find much more success, pleasure and rewards from their efforts. Being ungrateful limits a person's ability to get the most out of their efforts and their life. Being grateful maximizes your return on your actions.

Quotes
The more you are in a state of gratitude, the more you will attract things to be grateful for.
Unknown

Being content makes poor men rich: discontentment makes rich men poor.
Benjamin Franklin

Never let the things you want make you forget the things you have.
Unknown

Personal Experience
When you realize that things can come and go, you learn to become very grateful for the things you do have and how well you can live life without the things you do not have.

There are many things that I am grateful for, including the love received from my mother, the love I share with my wife, family, my good friends, good health, rewarding opportunities and my spiritual well being. What are you grateful for?

Recommended Book

The Grateful Life
Nina Lesowitz and Mary Beth Sammons

NOTES

_____

_____

_____

_____

_____

_____

_____

_____

_____

_____

_____

_____

_____

_____

_____

_____

_____

_____

_____

_____

_____

_____

_____

Forty Nine
Forgiveness

Forgiveness is what some people think they do for others. Not true. When someone wrongs you and you become upset or angry with them, you primarily incur the pain. Some people do not even get upset if you do not forgive them. They move on with their lives and or just ignore you.

Forgiveness is different from forgetting. One may not be able to forget, but forgiveness is a choice. It is your choice, and the sooner you make it the better you will feel. You can move on with your life and think positive thoughts rather than the have the negative feelings that one experiences from holding grudges or holding ill feelings.

Conclusion
Be quick to forgive so you can keep peace and positive thoughts in your life.

Quotes
It takes a strong person to say sorry and even stronger person to forgive.
Unknown

Forgiveness does not change the past, but enlarges the future.
Paul Boese

Personal Experience
There have been times in my life when I was slow to forgive, or in some cases, chose not to forgive. Later in life I learned that I am the only person that seems to be hurt when I choose not to forgive those who I feel have caused me pain. Now, I try to choose to forgive more quickly so I can feel better sooner.

It might be selfish, but it is one of those times being selfish is the right thing to do.

Recommended Book

Let It Go
T.D. Jakes

Fifty
Relationships/Friends

If someone tells you they have relationships all figured out, please be wary. We are in a constant learning curve when it comes to understanding relationships. The thing I do believe about all relationships is that they take patience, understanding, forgiveness, and compassion, and compromise, dedication of time, love and lots of work.

Some people say that you can usually count the number of true friends you have on one hand. This is true, however the limited number is probably due to the amount of effort a person makes to develop friendships. For people to be your friend, you have to dedicate time and energy to the relationship. Some do not choose to reciprocate. That is their choice. You must constantly pursue friendships, and those that do have more friends. Those who choose not to make the effort find themselves with fewer friends.

Conclusion
Relationships are challenging, but they are an essential and rewarding part of your life that deserves your constant attention. Friends can be plentiful based on your commitment to developing relationships. From these relationships come true friends that will enrich your life.

Quotes
The only way to have a friend is to be one.
Ralph Waldo Emerson

Wherever we are, it is our friends that make our world.
Henry Drummond

Walking with a friend in the dark is better than walking alone in the light.
Helen Keller

A real friend is one who walks in when the rest of the world walks out.
Walter Winchell

Personal Experiences

Sometimes you really don't know who your friends are. This works both ways. People you think are not your friends may truly be friends. Others you think may be your friends may not be true friends.

It may not be the number of friends you have that's important. What may be important is the fact that you as an individual have made the effort in your life to have true friends. This will bring you much satisfaction and will provide many friendships.

I have been pleasantly surprised to learn that some people who I thought weren't my friends actually are my friends. It's nice to know that when you give without expecting in return you may receive friendship unexpectedly.

Recommended Book

Men Are from Mars, Woman Are from Venus
John Gray

NOTES

Fifty One
Why Everybody Should Make $1 Million

OK, I just said it. If you are this far along in this book, my guess is that you have already decided that making million dollars is something everyone should at least consider. Actually, most people will make million dollars during their lifetime. It just varies how long it will take; some make it in a shorter time than others. Some people are offended by talking about money. That is okay. Those that are offended may have beliefs about money that lead them to their conclusion. Examples of such beliefs are: "Money won't make you happy." "Rich people are selfish." "I was born poor so I'll never have much money." "Life favors the rich so I won't ever be wealthy."

Your philosophy about money is what will determine if you ever accumulate much of it. Those with a negative philosophy will most likely be poor and those with a positive philosophy about money will most likely have enough to "make them happy."

Now, let me clear my conscience, I like money. I like it for all of the obvious reasons. It helps me provide food, shelter, education, health, travel, and entertainment for my family. It allows me to be an entrepreneur. It allows me to help others in many ways, including providing jobs, providing homes for people to live in and offices for people to work in. It also allows me to be generous, which not only helps those I give to, but helps me feel good about myself.

Eighty percent of millionaires are self made. That leaves only 20 percent that inherited their wealth. This proves that you can start with little and end up with a lot.

Conclusion
Whether you save $1 million or not will be determined by your philosophy. Once you develop a positive philosophy about money, you can work toward saving it, which will prove helpful in many ways. It is up to you.

Quotes

Successful people make money. It's not that people who make money become successful, but that successful people attract money. They bring success to what they do.
Wayne Dyer

Too many people spend money they haven't earned to buy things they don't want to impress people they don't like.
Will Smith

Remember, it's not about the money, it's about who you become from earning it.
Jim Rohn

The price of anything is the amount of life you exchange for it.
Henry David Thoreau

They say money won't make you happy, but everybody wants to find out for themselves.
Les Brown

Personal Experience

My life has been full of opportunity. Fortunately, with this opportunity I have not had to be concerned about having enough money for food, housing, education, and other provisions for my family.

However, a day does not go by without my realizing that others do have difficulty in acquiring enough money to meet their needs, wants and desires. There will probably always be those that have difficulty in having enough money to provide for the basics. This is part of life. It is an individual choice, one person at a time. What is your choice?

It gives me hope and pleasure to know that many people who start out with little ultimately find ways to obtain various types of wealth. This means that it is possible for those who start out with little to achieve personal and financial security.

My philosophy about money is quite simple. It is not about wanting or worshipping money. It is what can be obtained from providing value to others. For that value you provide to others, you receive things of value in return, like food, housing, security, safety, employment, education, friendship, self-esteem, confidence, achievement, and respect from others, pleasure, health, experiences, relationships, morality, creativity, self esteem and peace of mind. Those are all positives from having enough money.

My Uncle Gus lives in New York where he worked in the construction business as a blaster. The companies he worked for built roads and blasted mountainsides to construct roads through them. Uncle Gus' earnings from his lower middle class type job never provided him wealth directly. It did, however, allow him to use portions of his income to buy rental houses that he leased. He collected rent and made repairs after working many 10-hour days.

He took us fishing in a little Jon boat on the weekends and we thought he was rich. After all, we saw him accumulate seven houses that he has now owned for more than 50 years.

With a high school education, Uncle Gus became a millionaire and retired at 50 years old. He collected rents, bought a cabin in the Adirondacks, traveled to Florida in the winters. He wears white socks and slippers to the bank. The bank president calls him Mr. Panagiotis. There are a lot of Uncle Gus' out there.

Recommended Books

Financial Independence
Jim Rohn

The Magic of Thinking Big
David J. Schwartz PhD.

NOTES

_____

_____

_____

_____

_____

Fifty Two
Self-Esteem

Proper self-esteem is one characteristic that is vital to happiness. It is defined as, "confidence in one's own worth and abilities, self-respect." Some believe that you can have too much self-esteem, a greater sense of entitlement. With too much self-esteem one may not make the effort toward achievement, expecting something for nothing and ending up with little.

In life, we all have different experiences that affect our self-esteem. There are times when we feel good about ourselves and times that we do not. We have to recognize that it is our responsibility to work toward improving and maintaining ourselves and consequently our self-esteem. Do not wait for others to do it for you. Welcome the contribution others make, as you will gain from their encouragement, appreciation and respect.

Nothing will improve your self-esteem more than improving your individual ability to make and reach your own goals - no matter how small or how big. Learning and empowering yourself will constantly improve your self-esteem.

Conclusion
Having the right amount of self-esteem is most helpful in your pursuit of happiness. When you accomplish something for your self-esteem, your self-respect improves. This is not necessarily the case when others do it for you. This is one reason why it is so important for individuals to self improve, to reach goals and dreams on their own. Again, there is nothing wrong with a little help along the way. That is necessary too. When you bring the fish in the boat by yourself, it tastes better.

Quotes
Self-esteem is made up primarily of two things: feeling lovable and feeling capable.
Jack Canfield

To establish true self-esteem we must concentrate on our successes and forget abut the failures and the negatives.
Denis Whitley

Peace comes from within, do not seek it without.
Gautama Buddha

You're always with yourself, so you might as well enjoy the company.
Diane Von Furstenberg

Personal Experience

Looking back, I am not sure I had great self-esteem when I was in high school or when I was in college. Sure, it may have appeared that I did, but it was certainly a time when I, like most people, was building my self-esteem. Of course, over time a person's self-esteem may go up and down. At some point, after overcoming some difficulties or challenges by you, self-esteem improves. Once this happens, it sustains you and it carries you through more tough times. You learn to believe in yourself.

My opinion of my relationship with my father has changed over the years. I spent considerable time with my father working on projects at home and enjoying family outings, including boating each summer. However, at times I mistakenly felt my father ignored me or was too busy for me.

Now I realize that often he left me on my own to figure things out. He was much wiser than I gave him credit for. Many parents like me, with good intentions, go too far to help our children only to deprive them from doing things on their own and improving their self-esteem. It is surely a balance of both.

Recommended Books

Mindset, The Winners Attitude
Steve Williams

Feeling Good
David D. Burns M.D.

Fifty Three
Four Emotions to Evoke in Others to Create Influence and Win Friendships

Four emotions when evoked in others will assist you in both persuading them toward your objectives and/or creating positive relationships.

The first emotion is being uplifting. Smile, share an impressive hand-shake, compliment them, do something that is positive and uplifting.

Then create trust by using appropriate and positive body language.

Thirdly, show respect. Only after you have created trust will respect be real. This includes being respectful of the topic under discussion and in your dealings with an individual.

Show interest. Fourth and finally, if you want to influence people you have to show interest in them.

Conclusion
You can be most effective and have more influence on others if you take certain steps in earning the right to do so. Remember the four emotions, be uplifting, create trust, show respect and show interest.

Quote
You can make more friends in two months by becoming interested in other people than you can in two years by trying to get other people interested in you.
Dale Carnegie

Personal Experience
Reading the book *How to Win Friends and Influence People* at the age of 16 helped me with my career from an early age. A lot of doing the right things is common sense. We do not always make the conscious effort to do the right thing until we realize the importance of doing so. When we really want something, we tend to make better choices.

Recommended Book

Get the Edge
Tony Robbins

NOTES

_____

_____

_____

_____

_____

_____

_____

_____

_____

_____

_____

_____

_____

_____

_____

_____

_____

_____

_____

_____

_____

_____

_____

_____

Fifty Four
Seven Habits of Highly Successful People

1. They read - reading is to the mind as exercise is to the body.

2. Self-discipline is practiced. E.B. White, author of Charlotte's Web, said "A writer who waits for ideal conditions under which to work will die without putting a word on paper."

3. They keep calm and meditate.

4. They exercise regularly - it not only keeps you fit, but also makes you feel good by releasing endorphins. It makes your mind alert and teaches you discipline.

5. They persevere and practice hard - you can find shortcuts for everything in life, but you can never sidestep the hard work required to build the foundation of your goals.

6. They plan their day ahead. Plan the night before.

7. They invest in themselves by attending seminars on how to improve communication skills. They network with the best people in their field. They become the best in their field by learning more about it. (The above Seven Steps are outlined in Impulse for Men Success Magazine.)

Conclusion
If you want to hit where you're aiming, embrace these seven steps to help you get there.

Quotes
People often say that motivation doesn't last. Well, neither does bathing. That's why we recommend it daily.
Zig Ziglar

Personal Experience
I became aware of many of these steps early in life, but I often fail to keep them in practice. When I find myself behind the eight ball, I pull them out to get me through. If I could increase my use of these seven

habits, I know that I would reach a higher percentage of my goals sooner. How you develop these habits will determine the degree of success you will enjoy along your way toward achieving your goals.

Recommended Books

The Seven Habits of Highly Effective Teens
Stephen R. Covey

The 80/20 Rule
Richard Koch

NOTES

_____

_____

_____

_____

_____

_____

_____

_____

_____

_____

_____

_____

_____

_____

_____

_____

_____

_____

_____

_____

Fifty Five
Sales People

We all know sales people. We meet and associate with them daily as we work or shop. From shopping for small items like fast food or large items such as buying a car, we engage with sales people.

As in any profession or line of work, you have those that are just doing their job and those that stand out. You have those that have good reputations and those that are seen with disfavor. Historically, I think some sales people are known for being shady or wheelers and dealers. For example, many governmental regulations are put in place to protect the consumer against sales people who go beyond the truth in their representation of their products and services.

Regardless of all the potential past and future issues relating to the negative actions of sales people they are many times the most important part of any organization or group. Many times, they are the first person that you meet within any organization, the "face" of that organization. In addition, they are the persons that often spend more time with the customer than any other employee.

No company can survive without having an effective sales team. In fact, we are all sales people. Whether we are selling ourselves or the company we work for, we must be effective. In fact, many of the most successful sales people in an organization make more money than top executives and sometime more than an owner.

Being a sales person is difficult. Many times a sales person receives a small salary or none at all, relying commissions based on productivity. But there are many rewards. Personal satisfaction after reaching sales goals can be extremely rewarding, and financial rewards can be above many other employment opportunities. If one can adjust to the difficulties of being a sales person by saving during the good times and being patient during the slow times, being a professional sales person can be a rewarding and enjoyable profession.

Conclusion
Every organization is extremely pleased to have top sales performers

and often, as a result of success, sales people can demand much in return. Obtaining great salesmanship abilities and strengths will help with any endeavor, whether you are referred to as a sales person or not. In addition, if you choose this profession you may find yourself always in demand.

Quotes
You don't close a sale you open a relationship, if you want to build a long term successful enterprise.
Patricia Fripp

A good salesman is one who can sell himself before selling his products.
Unknown

Obstacles are necessary for success because in selling, as in all careers of importance, victory comes only after many struggles and countless defeats.
Og Mandino

Personal Experience
During my last year in college I had an interest in pursuing a career in the real estate profession so I attended a real estate sales representative class, took the Florida real estate salesman test and received my salesman license. I then moved to Houston and was employed in the construction management field. Regardless, I kept the license active in case I returned to Florida and obtained a job selling real estate. Finally, I decide to let it lapse because I thought I would not be returning to Florida. As luck would have it, shortly thereafter when the Texas economy bottomed out in 1982, I ended up back in Florida.

Although I never needed to personally have my license renewed, I became involved in selling real estate for more than 30 years while dealing with hundreds of sales people, both working directly with my organization and those working in other companies. We persevered through the slow times and enjoyed the good times. My training provided a good foundation in my relationship with many great sales people. I could not have accomplished much without them.

Recommended Book

The Greatest Salesman in the World
Og Mandino

Fifty Six
Join a Team

We all know that teamwork is required to be successful regardless of what profession or trade we choose. Working with others is something we should learn at a young age and continue to improve as we encounter greater challenges throughout life.

On every team, there usually are superstars that generate the most sales, the most points or the most touchdowns. They get most of the attention and make most of the money too. Some stay on the top of their professions longer than others do. Some never reach superstar status. Have you ever thought where the superstars would be if they had no blockers or did not have anyone to help them in practice to prepare for the big game?

All superstars know how important their teammates are to them and to the success of the team. All teams need players in different positions, doing different things, so the team can win. So being on a team is what is important, not necessarily being the superstar.

Conclusion
What is important is joining and being on a team. You might become a superstar or you may just help make a few superstars. Nothing is wrong with either one.

Quotes
Alone we can do so little: Together we can do so much.
Heller Keller

If you want to go fast then go alone. If you want to go far then go together.
African Proverb

Personal Experience
As a ninth grader, I was just average size and medium speed. I joined the junior varsity football team and finished the year playing just a couple of snaps. After one year, I chose not to remain on the team. At the time, I felt there was not much value in me taking the time to participate realizing that I would most likely not see many snaps as a junior either. I felt that I would suit up every day for practice, get my brains pushed in

and feel little value in my role on the team.

My son, Michael, also joined his football team in ninth grade. He too is just average size and medium speed. He was on second string and only played a couple snaps his first and second years. Prior to his senior year, I asked Michael if he was going to join the team. I knew it was tough practicing in the hot Florida sun everyday watching what you ate and spending countless hours in the weight room.

His answer surprised me. He said that although he knew he would not receive much time playing in the games, and that he knew that the players who were stronger, bigger, and faster than him would be playing most of the time, he still wanted to participate. He went on to say that he did not mind helping his teammates at practice and backing them up at the games. In fact, sometimes he felt that he had the best of both worlds. He was able to be part of the team without getting as many bumps and bruises from the games. In addition, he would be able to stay in shape by working out in the gym and running a few laps. You are wise beyond your years, son.

Recommended Books

Leaders Eat Last
Simon Sinek

The Magic Cup
Howard Behar

NOTES

Fifty Seven
Fishing

The sport fishing industry is one of the largest recreational industries in the United States. It is a $115 billion industry. There are more than 60 million anglers in the U.S. More than $46 billion is spent on fishing equipment and related items.

No wonder Bass Pro Shops are sprouting up everywhere. Sport fishing is bigger than golf and tennis combined. (They are $34 billion industries, combined.) Twice as many people fish than go to NFL games. There are 828,000 jobs, $35 billion in wages and over $15 billion in taxes generated from sport fishing.

What does all this mean? Why am I bringing this up? Something about fishing is relevant to our lives. With so many people, young and old, enjoying fishing there is something to be learned from this. Some people like to catch and release. Others like to catch what they can eat. There is respect among fisherman for the rules of what you can keep and a desire to protect the environment.

Conclusion
Fishing is so important and popular, perhaps because it teaches us many things and it provides many positive experiences in our lives. It teaches us patience, self-discipline, independence, teamwork, respect for the environment, attention to detail and many other things. It provides a place and a time to enrich our lives, whether young or old, by sharing and learning together.

Quotes
Give a man a fish and you feed him for a day. Teach a man to fish and you will feed him for a lifetime.
Maimonides

I will get you a fish if it takes every dime you got.
Capt. Jimmy Lozar, Islamorada, FL Fishing Guide

A bad day of fishing is better than a good day at work.
Unknown

Fishing provides that connection with the whole world. It gives you the opportunity of immersing yourself, turning back into you in a good way. It is a form of meditation, some form of communication with levels of yourself that are deeper than the ordinary self.
Ted Hughes

Many go fishing all their life without knowing that it is not fish they are after.
Henry David Thoreau

Personal Experiences
At an early age, around 7, my Uncle Bob would take me fishing and he would catch most of the fish. One day I asked, "Uncle Bob, why do you take me fishing because you catch most of the fish?" He said that the law of fishing was that 90 percent of the fish are caught by 10 percent of the anglers, then he joked and said that by bringing me along, I improved his chances.

My favorite day fishing was not quite fishing at all. My son, Michael, and I were at the Loreli, a restaurant and marina located in Islamorada, Florida, the fishing capital of the world. I operated the business from 2008-2010. President George H. Bush 41 fished out of the Loreli with a local captain almost every year. Knowing the president was about to arrive in a black SUV entourage, I asked my son to come over and meet the president. He did of course, and after the president visited with us for a few minutes and we got our pictures, President Bush and his fishing team departed for a day of bone fishing.

The next day when the President was about to arrive, my son was fishing nearby in the marina and I called over to my son and said, "Fish, (Michael's nickname) come on over, President Bush is about to arrive." He politely answered, "That's OK. I'm good."

I realized he had already met President Bush the day before and at 12 years of age, his love for fishing outweighed his desire to shake hands with the President a second time.

Recommended Book

Incredible and True Fishing Stories
Shawn Morey

Fifty Eight
Commitment

One can commit one's self at many levels. The lower your level of commitment, the less effective commitment will be as part of your life. Consequently, the more commitment, the more likely it will help you achieve what you are pursuing. Complete commitment comes when a person is convinced that what they are seeking absolutely will occur. Once fully committed you overcome both small obstacles and large ones.

Commitment is an important part in all personal relationships, business relationships and spiritual relationships. Commitment can be measured by how you spend your time and what you spend your time on. If you are committed to something, it takes time to work on it.

Relationships often fail because one or both parties really have not committed to one another. Without commitment to one another it's too easy to turn away and take an easier path. This is the same for pursuing a goal. If fully committed, you don't turn away and you begin finding solutions to whatever is interfering. Often, you can simply move forward believing that you will not stop until what you are seeking is obtained, and then answers do appear. This is because you are looking for them. Stop looking and you most likely you will not find them.

Conclusion
Use commitment to direct you in the direction toward what you want to achieve. Once you fully commit to something specific you will find steps that will take you where you want to be. Commitment means, there are no acceptable excuses.

Quotes
You may have to fight a battle more than once to win it.
Margaret Thatcher

Most people fail not because of lack of desire, but because of lack of commitment
Vince Lombardi

Stay committed to your decisions, but stay flexible in your approach.
Tony Robbins

Personal Experience
In my life I have enjoyed working on my commitment toward trying to improve individually, as well as making an effort to help others. In fact, as I have been successful in helping others I gained from my accomplishments. As I have improved I felt better toward myself.

At a young age I committed to the construction industry as I learned to build apartments and homes for people. Later I learned to develop office, commercial and industrial property that provided for new organizations and the expansion of existing companies. My commitment to build places for people to live, work, shop, retire and enjoy their lives grew stronger as I pleased those I served.

The building and development business has many obstacles and setbacks. Without a tremendous amount of commitment to my goals and objectives I would not have been able to enhance the lives of many as well as my own.

Recommended Book

It's Not Over Until You Win
Les Brown

NOTES

Fifty Nine
Final Thoughts

Life is good. You will encounter difficult times, so be prepared. Sacrifices are necessary. Self-development is not selfish. Self-development will improve your chances of success in many areas of your life, including dealing with others. It will provide you with additional enjoyment as you experience life's journeys.

Set your sail toward your goals and adjust them based on the wind. Do not seek to change the wind. Instead, change your sail. Take responsibility for yourself regardless of where you begin and what the circumstances are at any given time. This will increase your probability of finding and mastering your purpose. With purpose, you will have fuel to overcome all challenges.

Failures will teach you as much or more than your successes. You can manage fear as you succeed with those things you once feared. Positive relationships and having mentors will keep you on the right track, provide you with confidence and improve your self-esteem.

Reading, listening to audio books, watching self-improvement videos and attending seminars is something successful people do. Personal growth has no finish line. Being positive, having perseverance and being patient are attributes that must dominate your personality. Your value increases as you do more than what you are paid to do. When you believe in yourself at appropriate levels, you will help others believe in you. Do not let your success create enemies by boasting.

Develop your own personal philosophy and build a positive belief system. Do not wait to seek a spiritual relationship that will put you in the ultimate position to engage in life's journey. A deep spiritual relationship will humble you in the good times and carry you through the most troubling periods of your life. In addition, it will be with you during both your human state and beyond.

Giving to others not only helps others, but the good will bring you much in return. You attract good with good and you attract disappointment with negativity. Most of all, giving defines who you are and how you are remembered.

Your time on earth is limited so enjoy each day. We do not know which day will be our last. Take advantage of all the tools available to you to assist you in working hard on yourself first then on working hard at your job. Invest in yourself! If you do, you may never work a day in your life, and more importantly, you will be better to those around you.

Remember that people who overcome odds are those that realize:
- It is possible to do the right things
- It is all up to you, not others
- Life is going to be hard, so be prepared
- Those that overcome the odds know that it is worth it!

I hope this book will give you a jump-start on your life. I hope that it will thrust you ahead and help you stand out from your competition. It is meant to help you prepare for your future. It is now up to you! You will enjoy your voyage with your sail set toward your goals.

I urge you to refer back to these pages often, to remind yourself of the lessons I have learned. Use these tpoics as a compass to guide you as you build your future.

Please send me an email about your thoughts and reactions to this book, Live Smart, Start Young! You can be assured that we will appreciate your comments and contribution toward making our next addition of Live Smart, Start Young even more effective in assisting others to become personally and financially independent.

Visit our web page at www.livesmartstartyoung.com and email us at info@livesmartstartyoung.com

Thank You!
Live Smart, Start Young

CONGRATULATIONS

We hope you have enjoyed reading this book and believe that it will have a positive impact on you as well as others as you **Jump** start your life, **Stand** out from your competition and **Build** your future.

As you continue the pursuit of your dreams and explore your purpose in life we encourage you to participate in sharing this book with friends and family in an effort to assist others to become personally and financially independent.

You can accomplish this by making a donation to Live Smart, Start Young Scholarship Fund. The proceeds will be used to make more books available and to provide funds for scholarships to High School Students. The participants will be required to read the book and write a 500 word essay on what they learned and provide suggestions on how to make the next addition of Live Smart, Start Young more effective for its readers.

You can make a donation of any amount by utilizing the attached postage paid enveloped addressed to:
Live Smart, Start Young Student Scholarship Fund
333 S. Tamiami Trail, #205
Venice, FL 34285

Thank you for your consideration and remember "You can get whatever you want out of life if you help enough other people get what they want."